Reviving the Ruins

THE RECONSTRUCTION OF A FRACTURED SOUL

Deborah J. McCreary

Cover & interior design by Typewriter Creative Co.
Cover photo by Minoandriani #504609007 from Adobe Stock
Edited by Hillary Beth Trivette - HBT Editing

ISBN 979-8-9904364-0-4 (Paperback)
ISBN 979-8-9904364-1-1 (eBook)

Reverend Deborah J. McCreary is an amazing human being, and a child of God with a remarkable journey.

In this book, she shares that journey and gives voice to her experience of growing up in a challenging family system, as well as dealing with abuse and injustice of many kinds. The hope is that this book will be a comfort to many who share similar experiences, a guide to those just beginning their own journey, and hopefully a sliver of light and hope for folks who find themselves lost in similar places.

Ultimately, her book is a testament to hope, and the deep redeeming love of God. That Love has held her through all of it, and continues to transform her, as well those who trust in God's mercy.

Kudos to Deborah as well as the publishers of this book for bringing the story from birth into community.

—Rev. Celaine Bouma-Prediger, M.Div., Marriage
& Family Therapist, Spiritual Director

The Rev. Deborah J. McCreary is one of the most insightful, compassionate, and authentic people I know. I can only attribute this to the ways in which God has walked with her, and she has walked with God. Faith-filled and resilient, she is resourceful and tenacious in supporting the communities she serves. It was both a privilege and a delight to partner with her in congregational ministry.

—Rev. Brian P. Madison, Minister of
Word and Sacrament PC(USA)

Deborah J. McCreary is a daughter, sister, and mother. She carries her lived experiences into her pastoral work in Grand Rapids, Michigan. She sees the beauty of the world through art and traveling, and passionately advocates for justice. Knowing firsthand the impact a story can have; Deborah courageously offers her story of redemption with the invitation for others to consider and share their own story.

—SaraJane Herrboldt, M.A. in Counseling

Reverend Deborah J. McCreary is unapologetically a follower of Jesus Christ. Spending time in her presence you will notice her gifts of leadership, pastoring, advocating for social justice issues, as well as her ready pen for writing. Reverend McCreary paints pictures with her words and draws you into her story with raw realism and gentle grace.

She is an ordained minster in the Reformed Church in America. She has a Masters of Divinity degree from Western Theological Seminary and a Masters of Arts degree from Western Michigan University.

She has a passion to serve God – whether it is empowering a single mother, visiting someone who is sick or shut in, or being a prayer warrior for a friend. She makes each person feel valued and loved.

Those who know her well would describe her as brilliant, compassionate, genuine, direct, obedient to God's call, fun and adventurous. She is a mother, grandmother, sister, and friend who has weighted wisdom, infectious laughter, and a beautiful, gentle smile that lights up any room.

—Rev. Tamber Bustance, M.Div.

I dedicate this book to the woman who gave the 'Charge to the Minister' at my ordination.

She charged me "to be a teller of stories." She called me "a storyteller and a gifted preacher." I was told that I am "not just a teller of stories" but "also a holder of stories."

She became my spiritual director, my counselor/therapist, my sounding-board, and a trusted ally.

Thank you for listening to my story and holding it gently and carefully with love. You helped me to reframe my story, letting me know that it's *my* story, *I own it,* not another. You, along with Nova Bordelon, one of Ava DuVernay's characters in *Queen Sugar,* gave me permission not only to revisit it, but to retell it in new ways, with new awareness, new understanding, new healing, new forgiveness, and new grace.

It is with heartfelt love and gratitude that I dedicate this work to Rev. Celaine Bouma-Prediger who charged me to, "Tell the story of God's love and faithfulness."

This is part of that offering. My story. May He continue to bless it and me.

PRELUDE

This is the story of one woman's journey from innocence lost to a discovery of her true self in the loving arms of her Heavenly Father.

Why my story?

I'm like most of you.

Unknown. Ordinary. Nothing special.

I'm also unique. Gifted. Wrapped in grace.

I am the fourth of five children and the only girl.

I'm a daughter of the Most High God who has discovered that there is nothing that can't be forgiven and healed.

It's never too late.

God can, and does, make all things new.

He truly does redeem the time and give back what the locusts have stolen.

I thought maybe you might need to know.

INTRODUCTION

Do You Remember?

*"But the Helper, the Holy Spirit, whom the Father will send
in my name, he will teach you all things and bring to your
remembrance all that I have said to you." – John 14:26 NASB*

Memory is a strange animal. It consists of those events and perceptions that we self-recollect, combined with those that we piece together from shared stories we have repeatedly heard, many of which dredge up some faint impressions.

It is hugely impacted by our own skewed visual lens, the process of aging, and most dramatically by the experience of personal trauma.

The following is my recollection of my early life, including the interruptions of normalcy, which led to slipping down the rabbit hole, feeling trapped, swirling in the vortex, and finally leading to the journey back into the land of the living. Along the way I discovered how to hold deep loss, pain, and shame; in the end, I embraced my whole story as I discovered who I really am and the wonder of God's plan for me.

Flashback

*"...remember that at that time you were separate
from Christ..." – Ephesians 2:12a NIV*

The barrel of the rifle was quite long, slim, and almost close enough to reach out and touch. I remember standing there wondering why this crazy woman was pointing it at me while simultaneously scanning the room looking for my jacket, or sweater, or whatever the hell it was that I had left at the house and come to retrieve.

My friend, Roni, was in a heightened state of agitation and trying to get me to turn around and leave—without the article that I had come in pursuit of! That wouldn't have made sense to me even if I hadn't just smoked a joint on the way over there.

I had been kickin' it with JT. Shelia, the woman before me, was his longtime ex-girlfriend, with a few of his kids, who was now staying in his house during his absence.

It was nothing serious. He was slightly taller than me, about 5'10" or 5'11," and a medium to slender build. He wasn't particularly attractive, physically, or otherwise. He wasn't unattractive, but he wasn't a "hunk" either.

He just happened to be someone I ran into when I was bored, or more accurately, aimless, which was most of the time. JT was something to do, like reading a book or watching a movie. Nothing more.

He had just gone out to Portland, Oregon. I think he may have been bored too. One of his cousins had recently relocated there. It was an opportunity for him to try something different with minimum expense. I rode out with him, since I had never been across the top portion of the country, and then flew back.

I didn't want or care about him, her, or their kids. I simply wanted my personal item that I had inadvertently left at the house.

And even though I was high, it didn't seem rational that I

was required to stare down the barrel of a rifle in the process of recovering it.

Roni needed to either be quiet or wait in the car, as she was becoming annoying as well. Once Sheila finished playing out her drama, I retrieved my item and left.

What should have been a simple act, accomplished in 45 - 60 seconds, took several, long, drawn out minutes, in the presence of a long-barreled rifle, no less.

"What are you doing here? JT isn't here. He gave me the house," she snaps angrily.

"Yes, I know, that's wonderful! I apologize for bothering you. I just came to retrieve my sweater. I'll just grab it and be gone," I replied.

She grabs the rifle, levels it directly at me, and begins inching closer. "Have you seen it?" I ask. "It's brown and tan with large buttons."

"You need to leave," she snarls.

Roni begins tugging at me, saying, "Let's go!"

I ignore her. "Yes, we'll get out of your way in just a moment," I respond, as I gaze around the room for my sweater.

Sheila begins swinging the rifle back and forth. "I could blow you away right now," she says.

I ignored her thinking, *'Seriously? Who shoots someone because they want to recover a piece of clothing? You opened the door and let us in.'*

"Ah! There it is over there in the corner. Let me just grab it and we will be on our way. So sorry we bothered you."

Why was this drama necessary? What purpose did it serve? This is the insanity that infected my life after my brother's suicide. It only got worse following my father's death.

But I'm jumping ahead of the story – a story that began relatively normally. Really.

FORMATIVE YEARS

BEGINNINGS

"And God saw that the light was good; and God separated the light from the darkness." – Genesis 1:4 ESV

Mirror, Mirror on The Wall

"For now, we see in a mirror dimly, but then face to face; now I know in part, but then I will know fully just as I also have been fully known. – 1 Corinthians 13:12 ESV

My mother always seemed to enjoy sharing anecdotal tales about me with others, much to my chagrin. I'm not sure why. Maybe it comes with the territory of being the only girl among four brothers.

One of her favorite stories to tell was her discovery of me twisting and turning, inquisitively peering at myself in our full-length mirror.

"Debbie, what on earth are you doing? What are you looking at?"

The mirror was on the landing of the long, wooden staircase off the living room that led upstairs. Standing there in the open, one knew that they were at risk of being seen. If this had been an exercise in vanity, it would have been almost impossible to keep it private.

But I was only 6- or 7-years-old at the time. It was not vanity, but a moment of searching—an attempt to discover what others saw.

"People keep saying that I'm pretty. I'm trying to see it."

"Well," my mother responded, "pretty is as pretty does."

Now, that made sense to me.

I can remember, back in the heyday of my youthful 20-30's, men stopping and turning to look at me. My sister-in-law, Val, often pointed it out to me. I didn't pay much attention to it myself because I understood intuitively that it was meaningless.

Although I always understood that I was attractive, I have never used the adjective "pretty" to describe myself. Any fleeting moments that I felt pretty were a result of something kind or generous I had done for someone else. Yes, Mother's influence on me was greater than she ever imagined.

The truth is I was much more focused on those things that I considered shortcomings than any potential assets. We're conditioned that way, aren't we?

Who'll Take the Woman with the Skinny Legs?

"My frame was not hidden from you when I was made in the secret place, when I was woven together in the depths of the earth. Your eyes saw my unformed body…" – Psalm 139:15 NIV

What on earth possessed someone to come up with that song? I guess all of us females with the skinny legs. I was eleven and in the sixth grade, in 1967, when "Skinny Legs" first began playing on the radio.

It was a great upbeat tune! Joe Tex basically posed the question, who'll take the woman with the skinny legs? He responded that he would. This should have perhaps given me confidence that my skinny legs wouldn't matter, but alas, it did not. I would be entering junior high school soon and I was very self-conscious about my small frame.

My brother, David, loved teasing and taunting me with the song. I wonder if he ever realized how much damage it did to my small and fragile self-image.

For the record, my mother was what the R&B group, The Commodores, called a "Brick House," 36x24x36, with slim ankles and nice legs.

My dad, on the other hand, had pale, skinny legs. He used to tell me not to worry about my legs because they were shaped nicely and I have a pretty face. I was his little "Deb-Deb," so this encouragement was to be expected.

I remember being at a Lake Michigan beach one Sunday when I was probably in junior high. It was the first time that I can recall a boy talking and perhaps flirting with me. I was running up from the water on the sand with my float towards our family's blanket.

Out of the corner of my eye, I noticed a cute boy seemed to be approaching me. I immediately felt nervous. He reached me, smiled, and said, "Hi."

I dropped my gaze, and bashfully said, "Hello."

"What's your name? Do you come here often?" he asked.

"Yes, quite a bit," I responded. I felt awkward. I'm sure I was blushing as I turned away.

My dad noticed what had happened. He sweetly reminded me of how he had assured me that boys would soon begin noticing me. He also said, "Don't worry, in time you will become more comfortable with being around them and the exchanges of conversation."

So yes, I was favorably noticed despite my skinny legs. Skinny legs and little buds for a bosom. My shape was a throwback to Grandma Lulu, whose foam falsies I discovered on her bedroom dresser one day, much to her dismay.

These are not the greatest confidence builders for a young pre-teen. You would think I could at least get one or the other, right? If not the legs, then at least the breasts. But, as fate or genetics would have it, "No way, José." I think it was the beauty pageants and movies that made me so aware of my physical deficiencies, such that undressing for junior high gym class was embarrassing and excruciating.

My mother, bless her heart, was oblivious to my discomfort. Thank God for my next-door neighbor, Mrs. Green! She was probably a decade younger than my mother, down-to-earth, and had her own flat-chested daughter. She possessed both insight and empathy for my plight.

I don't recall how we even got on the topic, but one day, we ventured downtown together to Herpolsheimer's Department Store for a bra fitting.

Apparently, someone out there in the fashion world got it, because they had created little training bras for those of us who didn't have anything shaking around yet but were undressing in front of other folks who did.

It's amazing what a thin strip of material can do to boost your confidence and help you feel normal. Granted, all can still see that you're not filling out your sweater, but the psychological impact of wearing a bra in the locker room was momentous.

Thank you, Mrs. Green! I loved you twice as much for your thoughtfulness and understanding.

Congruent Duality

"So God created man in his own image..." – Genesis 1:27 NKJV

I know—you're thinking that title is an oxymoron. It isn't. Let me break it down for you.

I grew up in the age of playing games like jacks, hide & go

seek, kick the can, red light/green light, red rover, "Mother, may I?," jumping rope, and going on bike rides.

During the summer months, on any given day, you might find me outside in my makeshift tent on the side porch lost in my own fantasy world.

I mentioned that I was the only girl in a household with four boys and my father. That's a lot of testosterone. I was a well-balanced combination of both a stereotypical female and a girl with a variety of typically male interests.

You might catch me climbing trees or jumping roofs in the afternoon in my shorts and gym shoes. The following day you could encounter me in frills and patent leather shoes looking like a little princess. I was prissy and a tomboy all in one, trying to enjoy the best of both worlds.

As the only girl, I garnered a room to myself when we moved to Bates Street. The boys had a huge room featuring two sets of bunk beds, with no privacy. I had a princess bedroom set (without the canopy on the bed). I was your typical girl with stuffed animals, dolls, a dollhouse, and a slew of books. I didn't have a Barbie doll, though, because everyone else did. Instead, I had a Tammy doll—an early example of my desire to be a part of the group while at the same time being somewhat different.

I was generally on the perimeter, looking in. It's a slippery slope to navigate, especially if you are popular with adults and teachers, but not so much with your peers. Depending upon the group and/or the activity, a part of me might long to belong, or I could be totally indifferent. Sometimes I was invited in, other times I was kept on the outside, and still other times I elected to be aloof. This still proves to be true today.

I can remember a moment in ninth grade when I wanted the floor to open and swallow me. It was towards the end of the day. The teacher was chatting with the students about our hobbies and what we do on the weekends. Someone said something about skating and I foolishly made a comment.

One of my classmates said, "What are you talking about? You're not even allowed to go out anywhere in the evenings or during the weekend! Why are you sharing an opinion about something you haven't experienced?"

Mark lived a block away from me on the corner of Dolbee Ave. and Thomas St. Our families knew one another, so he knew that my parents were a little bit strict about where I could go. He also knew that my curfew was a bit earlier than those of other kids.

The truth is I wasn't a very good skater, even though I had earned my Girl Scout badge. I couldn't keep up and blend in with my peers skating, therefore, I didn't go. I wasn't allowed to go to any house parties yet, either.

I was cool with that because I didn't dance. I did the things with my friends that I enjoyed. However, it was horrifying being put on blast in front of the entire classroom! I could feel myself shrinking as if I had been zapped by an invisible ray. I mumbled something incoherent, looked down at my desk, cloaked in embarrassment, and pretended like I was no longer in the room as I anxiously awaited the ringing of the dismissal bell.

I would try to fit in at times, but often it was to no avail with the cool kids. Looking back, it's as if I was trying on a different friend from my block each summer in an attempt to find someone I connected with. The few girls around the corner that I clicked with were not acceptable choices in my mother's eyes. The irony is that the exposures she feared I would encounter with them came from a different, unexpected source. We'll get to that.

I was a victim of the current culture—movies, books, magazines, and TV shows. I was hooked on mysteries and fantasy love stories. As I got older, I wanted to be the damsel in distress rescued by the knight in shining armor or Cinderella scooped up by the prince.

TURNING POINTS

"Remember the days of old; consider the years of many generations…" – Deuteronomy 32:7a ESV

Beginning Discoveries

"At the heights overlooking the road, at the crossroads, she takes her stand." – Proverbs 8:2 CSB

The summer after kindergarten we moved into a working middle-class, White, Christian Reformed neighborhood. Or that's how it was for the first few years until the White flight began.

"DEBBIE, DEBBIE!" Mary called out at the top of her lungs, standing on the sidewalk, directly in front of our house. We were on the corner of Bates Street and Dolbee Avenue. She lived right around the corner, adjacent to our driveway on Dolbee.

"Your little White girlfriend is out there yelling for you again," my brother David said, both informing and teasing me in the same breath. Mary was not allowed to come inside our house. At the time I'm not sure if I thought about or analyzed why not. In retrospect, most certainly it was because of all those Black boys in there. A dark, looming threat in her parents' minds, I'm sure.

It was probably a stretch for her parents to even let her play with me, but they did. And I was allowed inside their home, being deemed safe and harmless, no doubt. Looking back on it, their home was not as large, or nice, as ours. I think she had two older siblings. So, they probably didn't need a larger home.

I distinctly remember her eating butter and sugar sandwiches and wondering, *"Where's the meat?"* Or, at least some peanut butter & jelly. I certainly considered us to be better off than them.

We played with our dolls, jacks, jump ropes—all the regular kid stuff—until Mary's family moved away within the first two years of our joining the neighborhood. I never saw her again.

They were part of the White flight that was to become massive over the next few years, making room for even more Black families to come in, which was the reason they were moving out, a self-perpetuating action.

What Are You?

"I praise you because I am beautifully and wonderfully made…" – Psalm 139:14 NIV

I was maybe seven or eight and my younger brother, Albert (aka. AJ), two or three when we walked together down Dolbee hill to Princess Bakery on Franklin Street. I remember the two ladies working there, oohing and aahing as we walked in, saying how cute we were. Then they asked, "What are you?"

I'm sure that I tilted my head slightly to look at them as I pondered their question. *"Clearly, I'm a girl and he's a boy, so just what is it that you're really asking me?"*

"Excuse me?" I ventured.

"What are you? Are you Indian?" they inquired. I was aware that I had a little bit of Cherokee in me—I even had a porcelain doll at home in her native dress—but somehow, I knew that wasn't what they meant. Yes, even that young my antenna was finely tuned.

"Where do you come from?" They were thinking we were from India, Pakistan, or some far off Middle Eastern country. "You're both so beautiful!"

"Ok, I get it," I thought. *"You're commenting on our skin color and the texture of our hair."*

"We live up the street and around the corner," I replied. "We'd like to get a couple of donuts, please. Thank you."

The Double Whammy

"You are altogether beautiful, my love; there is no flaw in you." – Song of Solomon 4:7 ESV

I turned 16 just after my junior year of high school started. I decided that I wanted to get a job and have my own money. My mother deferred this type of decision to my father. He objected. "School is your job. You don't need another one," was his response.

"Yes, I know," I responded. "I'm excelling at that job. I'm getting A's and a couple of B's, plus participating in extracurricular activities. I'm pretty sure I can handle a second, part-time job. Could I try it out and see, please?"

Dad thought about it for a few moments and replied, "Just a few hours per week."

"Great! Thank you," I beamed!

I was familiar with department stores from hanging out at Wurzburg's where mom worked. I decided I would work at Herpolsheimer's. I was in school during the week, so I would have to go downtown on a Saturday morning. I dressed up, putting on a skirt with an attractive sweater set. I wore pantyhose with my little pumps. I put on just a touch of makeup to look more mature. I took the bus downtown to apply for a position. Now mind you, I had no idea if they were hiring. I had just decided I wanted to work.

I arrived at the store and took the escalator up to the second floor where the personnel office was located. Taking a deep breath to calm my nerves, I approached the woman at the desk. I introduced myself and stated that I was interested in applying for a part-time position. The woman politely told me that they currently didn't have any openings. I thanked her and turned to leave.

Before I could walk off, I saw an attractive, petite woman, smiling sweetly as she approached me. It almost seemed like she was skipping, or taking a little hop, with her lively approach; she had a bounce in her step. "Hello. My name is Dorothy. I'm the manager of the women's clothing department. I saw you when you first came in. Would you like to work in my department? My bridal consultant is currently on a short leave of absence. You could fill in for her, but once she returns you will have to work in women's dresses."

I wasn't excited about the older women's dresses, but I was delighted to get hired. I said, "Yes!"

One day an older woman came in looking for a simple house dress. She wanted assistance, but not from me. There weren't any White clerks on the floor at that moment. I politely invited her to use the fitting room at her discretion and left her alone. She was frustrated at not finding something she liked.

Without saying anything, I began gathering a few things to show her. I hung them right outside her dressing room so that she could try them on. She found a couple things she liked and was very grateful. She began talking to me, asking how the dress looked on her. I was able to compliment her and ask a couple of questions to get a more complete idea of what she was looking for.

In that moment, I became her personal clerk. My skin color no longer mattered. Instead, she saw my patience, kindness, and my eye for choosing something that suited her and wasn't overpriced.

She learned my schedule, and shopped only on the days I was working. She would patiently wait for me if I was assisting another customer, letting the other clerks know that only I could serve her.

Daddy got over the fact of me working part time, and I was reminded that our prejudices and differences begin to fall away when we enter relationships with one another. I constantly need the reminder because as I'll share shortly, I wanted to be a Black Panther, a militant, down for the cause. I loved Huey P. Newton! He, along with Bobby Seale, started the organization in Oakland, CA as a campaign for equality, justice, and equity for our people. I was impressed that they openly carried weapons as a message to the police force that Black men are tired of being shot down like prey. I appreciated how they addressed practical needs in the community such as establishing learning centers for youth, food programs, and health clinics.

The irony was that as my interactions, at work, were opening the older White woman's worldview towards people of color, my own outlook was shrinking. Although I still hung out with a varied crowd at school, that was beginning to shift. My growing awareness of bigotry and discrimination, watching the Civil Rights Movement take form and stand up for Brown and Black people, along with my ever-increasing reading list caused my openness to White people to drastically decline. I began to stereotype them in the same way I felt they treated people of color. I grouped them together, labeling them all as being racist, seeing the few who weren't as the exceptions. For example, my brother Bruce dated a White woman, whom I liked and hung out with when they came to visit. This change in my beliefs and attitude was still new at this point. I was inconsistent with my relationships.

I met someone named Mary at the Ottawa Hills High School basketball games. We sat together at our older brothers' games from the time we were in 5th through 8th grade. Our home games were played at Christian High School's gymnasium. They had a stack of exercise floor mats in the corner on the balcony. This was our designated spot to meet up and watch the games.

I was in the hot seat this class session. Mary, who was White, and whom I did not hang around with at school despite our basketball days, decided to take advantage of me being in the chair.

She raised her hand to ask a question. "What caused you to change from the way you were back when we watched the basketball games together? You seemed more open and friendly back then. Now it seems that you don't like White people very much."

I replied, "I imagine it has something to do with the effect of growing up and learning how much racism exists and how it impacts my people."

I could see her bewilderment and hurt, but I didn't have the grace to offer her at that time.

As God would have it that opportunity presented itself during a "random" encounter decades later when I was in seminary.

There was too much raw pain and frustration to express in a few short sentences from the hot seat in class to help her understand the shift that had taken place within me.

Would she even understand or appreciate how painfully weary it is to be mistreated and excluded based upon one's ethnicity? It's exhausting not to be treated as a human being. I'm not sure if White people get it. We don't choose our skin color. Well, a few might excessively bleach or tan, but most of us live in the skin shade we are born with.

I understand the lie that color matters. An insidious evil has been perpetrated by dominant culture to divide Black and Brown people through an illusion of acceptance by White America based upon the lightness or darkness of our skin tones.

I'm aware of the history of the "field nigger" and the "house nigger." Generally, only those with a lighter skin complexion were chosen to work inside "Master's big-house." They received a few more material comforts than their darker skinned compadres who did all the hard manual labor in the fields.

Even once slavery ended, it became apparent that this color bias was entrenched in society at large. Employment opportunities and social engagements for people of color were frequently determined by the amount of melanin we possessed. It is still prevalent due to the unconscious prejudice and bias that is deeply ingrained into the fabric of our lives.

The depth of this brainwashing is so prevalent amongst Black Americans that even today it manifests in our society. I still encounter it as a mature, grown-assed woman. It's unbelievable! Yet, in a way it is totally understandable, as the tentacles of racism are pervasive throughout every aspect of life. My lighter complexion and the less coarse texture of my hair has always been held against me with the false projection that I must consider myself to be better than others who are darker.

Indeed, Mr. Henry confessed as much when he told me he was sorry for allowing staff at the Grand Rapids, Gerald R. Ford Job Corps Center to bully and abuse me. He thought I was "stuck up," as Black folks say, and therefore deserving of the mistreatment, I guess.

Much later, after the fact, declaring he was surprised I never sued the Center for all its various misconduct, he said, "McCreary, you're OK."

"Yes, Negro, I know," I thought.

We continue to perpetuate this madness with our young girls and boys, as if they don't already have enough challenges. They struggle with growing up in an amoral culture, amidst the violence, broken educational systems, and lack of opportunities.

I wonder how many of our girls of color are still drawn to the blonde, blue-eyed dolls, rather than dolls that reflect their images, as noted in psychological studies decades ago.

If you are not familiar, the Clark Doll Test was a psychological experiment that began in the US in the 1940s and has since been repeated numerous times. It was devised by Psychologists Kenneth and Mamie Clark to study children's attitudes toward race and their self-image. They used four dolls, identical except for color, to test children's racial perceptions.

The children between the ages of three and seven were asked to identify both the race of the dolls and which color doll they prefer. They all preferred the White doll. It was concluded that "prejudice, discrimination, and segregation" created a feeling of inferiority among African-American children and damaged their self-esteem. (Kennethclark.commons.gc.cuny.edu/the doll-study/)

I know that our young black boys are still being railroaded in school, over-disciplined, expelled, and disproportionately assigned to special education classes. Once they hit the third grade, many are written-off, primed to become part of the juvenile correctional system, and our for-profit prison system begins counting beds to incarcerate them.

Our words proclaim our freedom and evolution while our actions reveal the depth of the disillusionment that continues to separate and divide us as a people.

We, in our brainwashed state, are like crabs in a barrel, too often pulling one another down instead of unifying and support-ing one another in our quest for equity and acceptance. "Black Lives Matter" needs to be joined with a resurgence of "I'm Black and I'm Proud," so that not only do we embrace our natural hair and our Afro-centric clothing and jewelry, but we truly accept ourselves in all our beautiful array of shades of Blackness.

I think one generally accepts the advantages while at the same time resenting the fact that they exist. At least that was my experience in my earlier years. I have walked through the doors that my light skin has opened, interviewed with my hair look-ing "presentable," and accepted the positions that my "proper" English gave me access to before flaunting my "Afro" and my fully, beautiful, Black self!

Thank God I have lived to see positive movements both within our ethnic group and larger society as it is forced to embrace the Crown Act and other equity policies.

The CROWN Act was created in 2019 by Dove and the CROWN Coalition to ensure protection against discrimination based on race-based hairstyles. It provides protection to hair texture and styles such as braids, locs, twists, and knots in the workplace and public schools. Twenty-four states have adopted the law, as of July 2023, including Michigan.

Yet, there remains so much more to do. It is such a vicious, never-ending cycle.

Rude Awakening

"If we claim to have fellowship with him and yet walk in the darkness, we lie and do not live out the truth." – 1 John 1:6 NIV

I was seven years old, almost eight, the spring that newscasters Chet Huntley and David Brinkley brought Governor Bull Conner's fire hoses and police dogs attacking children and grown folks down in Alabama directly into our living room. I couldn't make sense of what my eyes were witnessing. Of course, I grew up hearing stories about the South and how racism was worse down there. And, I had heard comments about being careful as we drove through Howell, Michigan on the way to my grandmother's house in Ann Arbor because of the Klan.

This was different. This was not just hearing words; this was watching live TV with its pictures, this unconscionable response to the Birmingham protests. This was vile, livid, bold, and brazen hatred on display in Alabama.

This was the stuff that birthed slavery and fueled Jim Crow laws, led to the formation of Citizen Councils and the Ku Klux Klan, and now embraces the "Big Lie," that is, conspiracy theories (The "Big Lie" is the false narrative being shared by Donald Trump and his supporters that he won the last presidential election, when in fact he did not). It inspired the insurrection at the

Capital, and longs for the "good old days" when Jim Crow was alive, well, and accepted as the norm. Indeed, it is the poison of which some political leadership drink and in which many evangelicals now wallow.

New and real to me in ways that I had not recognized or previously known, it touched me. Awakened me. Stirred curiosity in me while also causing me to begin questioning the nature of people and why God allowed things to be so. I began searching at the library for books written by people who looked like me. I initially stumbled upon Phyliss Wheatley, Paul Lawrence Dunbar, and Langston Hughes.

I was delighted to find poetry written by a Black woman. Although I confess that initially there was a struggle with Wheatley's use of language. I had to learn the rhythm of her cadence and the structure of her words. She was an enslaved woman from West Africa who lived in Boston. Her thoughts shared the strength and resolve of people even while enduring unfathomable life situations. Her writings were so well done that she was initially accused of falsely claiming the works of a White person. She proved them wrong.

I held Paul Lawrence Dunbar with the same high esteem as I did Wheatley. He was the son of formerly enslaved parents, growing up after the Civil, and eventually attending Howard University. One of his most famous poems is, "We Wear the Mask." It resonated with me even as a middle-schooler because I was already seeing the "roles" people of color often enacted engaging with White folks. It was quite prominent whenever we traveled to Point Pleasant Beach, New Jersey to visit my grandma Lulu. Her interactions and conversation with the White folks she worked for was remarkably different from her relaxed banter with us. People of color seemed to always be on guard with Whites. They were not to be trusted. The words that were spoken were often short and to the point, whereas speaking among one's "own" people allowed folks to relax and be light-hearted.

Hughes was a giant in the literary world. He may be best known for his short poem, "I, too." He is more contemporary than the other two, as such his style of language is easier to read. He, too, paints vivid pictures of Black American lives with his words.

These three were my opening to a broad range of Black writers, male and female, of poetry, fiction, and non-fiction. They not only exposed the world to me, but shared depths, insights, and understanding with a curious young student trying to make sense of her country, which was often on fire.

I'm Included in the Exclusion

"Blessed are you when people hate you, and when they exclude you, revile you, and defame you on account of the Son of Man." – Luke 6:22 NRSV

That fall I entered the third grade. At some point during that year, I experienced my first up close and personal encounter with bigotry and prejudice. One of my classroom friends had a birthday party. She was from a Middle Eastern country. Her father, upon learning that I was Black, forbade her to invite me.

She stood her ground. I went to the party. I was treated like the other guests and had a good time. I still remember the game of carrying marshmallows across the room on a spoon.

The irony lies in the fact that my skin coloring was the same as theirs. My hair was the same length as his daughter's and almost the same texture. All of which begs the question, what is Blackness, and why do we try to discriminate and segregate ourselves?

The question is rhetorical, right? We know the answer.

BEGINNING EXPLORATIONS

"Hear, my son, your father's instruction, and forsake not your mother's teaching, for they are a graceful garland for your head and pendants for your neck." – Proverbs 1:8-9 ESV

Family Details

"Children's children are a crown to the aged, and parents are the pride of their children." – Proverbs 17:6 NIV

I grew up in a family that was politically active. During election seasons, I can remember walking the neighborhoods, going door-to-door, passing out pamphlets with my dad and encouraging folks to get out and vote. My father was also proud to be on the union bargaining committee at Kelvinator where he was employed as an inspector.

My maternal grandmother was "the help" until diagnosed with cancer and coming to live with us when I was in 7th or 8th grade.

I loved coming home from school and just standing in the doorway as the aromas wafted throughout the house, offering a warm welcome. I remember bowls holding precious dough, each covered with a dish towel, sitting on the heat registers around the house to speed up the process of the yeast rising.

Grandma Lulu was a master chef. Every meal was a delight, not to speak of her desserts. Oh, my!

I would always ask. "What's for dinner?" knowing that she wasn't going to tell me. She did not like folks to ask. You had to wait and see. On days when I was feeling mischievous, I would try to peek in the oven or lift the lids on pots.

One of my favorite memories is her chasing me around the dining room table brandishing a wooden spoon. "Debbie, you stop running. Stop laughing! I'm going to tell your mother. You come here!"

There was no way she could catch me. She was livid, but that picture seared in my mind is so funny! I can see her still today with her dancing eyes and turned up lips. Hilarious! God, I love that woman!

We visited her a few times during summer vacations prior to her moving in with us. Twice I spent weeks with her at the "Big House" on the river in Point Pleasant Beach, New Jersey, where she lived and worked just a short walk from the ocean.

My mother was an only child, born in Philadelphia, PA. She grew up in this mostly White enclave and was the only person of color in her high school class. She knew, from firsthand experience, the reality of both worlds, traversing them both with grace.

Her father was abusive towards Grandma. One day while he was at work, she backed their belongings, and moved to New Jersey. I don't know how old my mother was when that happened.

Grandma Lulu had brothers living in Point Pleasant Beach, Newark, and East & West Orange which were suburbs of Newark, New Jersey. This was how Grandma secured the job working for the Wattles as their live-in help and house manager.

I was nine when I flew East my very first time, and solo, at that! I confess, I enjoyed being spoiled.

On Sundays, we went to the Baptist Church that Grandma

Lulu attended. This allowed me to experience a freer form of worship with amazing singing. After service, we often visited various relatives.

I looked forward to Thursdays, which was grandma's other day off. We would venture off to Asbury Park or Newark and the Oranges. We ate in nice restaurants, shopped, and I always took along my sneakers or sandals for the amusement rides on the boardwalk we would visit before taking the train back home.

I discovered Troll dolls one summer afternoon on the boardwalk at the Atlantic Ocean in Asbury Park. I was immediately enamored with them. I thought they were the cutest, little, unusual things! Clearly, I was right because they now even have their own movies! I knew it the moment I saw one. I began collecting them each time we visited the boardwalk. I still have my favorite one stored in my treasure box.

The first time I encountered the dolls I excitedly showed them to Grandma Lulu, who was piqued by my pronouncement that their faces resembled hers with their turned-up lips. I was expressing my fondness for her, but she didn't receive it as such, thinking I was mocking how she looked. Our self-images haunt us well into our adult life, maybe even to the grave.

It was relaxing lying on the front lawn's grass embankment, above the sandy beach and river, watching the sailboat races. I loved falling asleep listening to the waves hitting shore, rolling out of bed in the morning, and taking a dip in the river before breakfast.

It felt natural to me that Grandma would "draw my bath," getting the temperature of the water just right each time. I was abruptly brought back down to earth upon returning home, waiting for Mom to start my bath, which did not happen.

"Alright princess, you're back home in the Midwest. The fairy tale life is over now," Mom would remind me, as she chuckled and shook her head.

Unbeknownst to me at the time, it was all part of my education on this social construct we call race, and a glance into the differences of socio-economic status.

My paternal grandmother did laundry for University of Michigan professors, doctors, and lawyers, all of whom were White folks. She was actively engaged in civil rights and politics—to the extent that she was invited to President Kennedy's inauguration. Family folklore says that she was the first person of color to purchase a home in Ann Arbor, Michigan and that she was the first to serve on the City Council there.

The house we grew up in on Bates Street was in a protected all-White district when my parents purchased it. There was only one Black family in a six-block area. My father had served in World War II and was eligible for financing under the GI Bill. Yet, the bank was refusing the sale due to the real estate practice of red-lining—mapping out the city's neighborhoods to indicate where people of color would be permitted to live—and not live.

A prominent Jew who managed Wurzburg's, where my mother worked, and a wealthy White couple, who owned a substantial business in the city and knew my parents through the Grand Rapids chapter of the National Urban League, interceded on behalf of my parents and insisted that the bank approve the loan.

Segregation, discrimination, and White privilege were conversational topics in our house. We were taught our history, told not to give White folks any information on the phone, and reminded that no one was any better than we were.

The Riots

"Fools give full vent to their rage, but the wise bring calm in the end." – Proverbs 29:11 NIV

The summer before my twelfth birthday, we drove out East to visit Grandma. I stayed behind with her for a few weeks.

One Thursday, we took the train up to Newark to shop and visit some of our relatives in East Orange, as we were prone to do on her day off. Only this time was different—the 1967 riots had just occurred.

Upon departing the train station and stepping out to catch a cab, we were almost run over by a cabbie who spewed something racist at us, refusing to stop and give us a lift. Folks in the department stores seemed on edge and not very friendly.

We cut the shopping trip short, grabbed lunch, and headed over to my cousin Evelyn's to visit and hear an account of what had been taking place over the last month. The general frustrations with the lack of employment opportunities and all the inequalities came to a head following an act of police brutality against a Black man, resulting in several days of rioting.

1967 was a long, hot summer with riots breaking out around the country. They even had a riot in Grand Rapids while I was out East, burning down 33 homes over the course of three days. This was the year before Dr. King's assassination and the Holy Week Uprising that followed.

I was entering junior high that fall and my reading list began to change. The riots stirred something in me just as the dogs and hoses had. I read Richard Wright's Native Son, Ralph Ellison's *Invisible Man, The Spook Who Sat by the Door* by Sam Greenlee, Claude Brown's *Manchild in the Promised Land,* and the *Autobiography of Malcolm X,* just to name a few.

By ninth grade I had read everything I was aware of written by, or about, one of the Black Panthers. I still loved Huey P. Newton. I was proud that my A+ paper on the Panthers garnered an A- for my brother, David, in his freshman class at Western Michigan University.

The reality of our Black history and the current climate compelled a desire in me to become a Black Panther member. I was, as we say today, "Woke." Or, at least, awakening. This awareness had been birthed when I was in third and fourth grades as I watched the marches, sit-ins, and ferocious attacks against people of color.

But the truth was, I didn't know of anything in ninth grade that I was willing to die for. In my innocent mind I fell short. Not a Black Panther's heart and commitment after all.

This was the beginning stage of a Black consciousness that would be expanded both through future readings, as well as the classes I would take my first two years at the University of Michigan.

As I've grown in awareness and wisdom over the years, I have continued to struggle defining what activism looks like for me, and what the balance is incorporating it into my everyday life flow.

In some ways I feel the same as I did at age 14, as if I am taking the easy road, and that I am never doing enough for the cause of justice and equity.

NOT SO NORMAL

"Before I formed you in the womb I knew you, and before you were born I consecrated you; I appointed you a prophet to the nations." – Jeremiah 1:5 ESV

The Beginning Tilt

"Come to me, all you who are weary and burdened, and I will give you rest." – Matthew 11:28 NIV

What we experience day in and day out, or with intermittent frequency throughout the year, is recognized as "our normal." I believe this is true whether you live like the families in *Leave it to Beaver* and *The Cosby Show,* or *Good Times* and *Sanford and Son.* For better or worse, what we experience repeatedly becomes our norm. It is also true that we almost intuitively know when our "normal" is skewed or off-course from that of society at large.

Let me give you an example. My father, who possessed a high IQ and a brilliant mind, was extremely well-read and knowledgeable. He also just so happened to be manic-depressive, what we now call bipolar.

Most of my memories of him consist of "normal" times and

behaviors to a large enough degree that I grew up feeling safe and secure.

However, the extremes of mania and deep depression do leave an indelible mark on those exposed to it, even intermittently. And, there were also times when he was drinking heavily and his actions were unpredictable.

I remember walking up the slope of Dolbee Avenue from Franklin Street towards our house there on the corner of Bates and Dolbee. I was probably 13- or 14-years-old. Dad was sitting on the porch. He saw me approaching. He was drunk and began calling out to me. He was loud and slurring his words. He was yelling out "compliments." I was mortified, humiliated, angry, and sad all in the same moment. "Take your drunken self into the house! Stop embarrassing us! Why don't you lock yourself in your room again and leave us alone," I shouted. "Stop making life a living hell for us."

Once, during my elementary years, my father locked himself in his bedroom for a period of weeks. My memory is a bit fuzzy, so it may have been as many as seven, and I'm almost certain that even if it wasn't that long, it was well over a month.

At any rate, he was missing in action long enough for one of the neighborhood kids to notice and inquire where he was. Because, after all, it was not "normal" for one's father to drop off the face of the earth. For me, his behavior, while certainly extended to an extreme this time, was not new. I lived with the effects of his depression and his isolation from time to time. It was normal to me.

Yet, I immediately knew upon being questioned that my friend would not see it as such. So, I lied. "Oh, he's been working out of town during the week and coming home sometimes on the weekend," I shared. "You probably just missed seeing him since he comes and goes so quickly." There was no known reason for my neighbor to think we were peculiar, so he believed my explanation.

My father would come out and roam around the house during the hours when we were sleeping. Once his depression began to lift, he would begin a slow process of re-entry into the world. This resurfacing consisted of making brief appearances, eventually attending to his personal hygiene—cutting his hair, shaving off his beard—and then finally, full emergence and a return to normal.

A More Complete Description

"And he will turn the hearts of the fathers to their children and the hearts of children to their fathers." – Malachi 4:6 ESV

I adored my dad growing up. I was Daddy's girl. Most of the time I was spoiled and could get what I wanted from him—be it time, attention, or some material item.

Sometimes the entire family trekked to the beach during the summer months. Dad loved the water, as do I. Other times, Mom would pack up a picnic lunch on Sundays and daddy would take the kids to the park or beach, giving her a day off.

Some Sundays we would all pile into the car, not knowing where we were going. It was amazing how many little towns, lakes, and rivers he knew around Michigan.

We had previously toured the Kellogg's cereal company and had a sweet treat of vanilla ice cream with Fruit Loops on top at the end of the visit.

This time we visited the arboretum which was lovely! We then pulled up to this very small museum housed in a large, old home. We found ourselves entering the Kingman Museum, which has since been relocated to a newer, larger facility.

The museum had a variety of historical artifacts reflective of Michigan's history and various changes through the decades. What captured my attention was a display in the health and science section. It was the first time I saw a small fetus in a jar. You could tell that the embryo was the beginning stage of a new life. It was fascinating to see!

We had an interesting conversation on the way home about humans, animals, birds, and mammals lives' and reproduction. Dad was agnostic so he saw life more from an evolutionary viewpoint rather than seeing life as created by God. What struck me was his example of when we crack an egg to cook; the white spot we see on the egg yolk is what becomes the embryo that becomes the little chick. He compared it to the tiny embryo that we saw in the museum and broke down the stages of development. I loved it when we went exploring!

My father was influential at other times in my education. As I got older, my mother would often raise an objection to a particular book I was reading, stating that I was too young for the topic or language. My father always countered that one is never too young for what draws their interest, so I was always allowed to read whatever I wanted. My father most likely had previously read anything I was reading. If not, he would make a point to read the selection. Later, he would engage in conversations with me about the books to hear my thoughts, and to discuss any questions I might have.

I later learned that he had similar check-in conversations with my brothers when they were held captive in his barber chair, listening to him pontificate about the state of the world and being quizzed about their lives in general.

With the exceptions of his denying me a new pair of jeans to wear to a football game in 9th grade, his failure to attend my Cotillion Ball's father-daughter dance, and his absence at my senior graduation—all part of the shocks and vibrations I experienced due to his mental illness—daddy was generally present in a positive way for me.

I realize I am sharing these in a light-handed manner, as if they were not significant. That is not at all the case. By the time of the

Cotillion Ball, I was unsure and nervous about his conversation and behavior such that I would have been uncomfortable having him escort me. Yet, it still was embarrassing having Mr. Porter stand in as a substitute for my father at the event when all the other girls had their dads there.

Warner and Edna Porter were my parents' best friends and like family. Despite any discomfort, I was grateful to have him attend our dance lessons and the ball with me.

The truth is at a deep level there is still a part of me that is wounded from Dad not being present at my graduation. I don't know if he attended my younger brother's graduation, but he certainly attended my older brothers' events.

This is true even though I now understand that his mental illness was becoming progressively worse as he aged. Things he had the capacity to do for my brothers during his younger years slipped away from him.

Looking up into the stands I saw my mother, siblings, and friends. However, being "Daddy's girl," his absence caused me to feel like I was not important – I was insignificant. It contributed to my internal conflict between "knowing" I was loved as opposed to "feeling" loved.

My mind understood, but my heart was deeply scarred. I'm sure that on an unconscious level, it is part of what caused me to always seek desire and acceptance from men until I surrendered to the Lord.

Curiosity Killed the Cat

"My flesh and my heart may fail; but God is the strength of my heart, and my portion forever." – Psalm 73:26 NIV

I was eight or nine when Daddy locked himself in his room for the extended period. I knew that he was a voracious reader. I knew that from time to time, he mentioned working on his book. What I didn't know and couldn't fathom was what on earth he could possibly be doing holed up in that room day in and day out, week after week.

What was in there?

Well, I had a plan to find out. As soon as he began leaving the room to resume some normal activity, I was going to sneak in there and look. I made my trek down to Ooms Hardware store, two blocks from our house, and purchased a skeleton key. And I waited.

Finally, the day arrived. No one was around. I quietly slipped my special key in the door, turned the handle, and behold, I entered the room of chaos.

Dad had yet to begin the process of cleaning up, so there were dishes and things strewn about. Books were stacked precariously on shelves and also around the perimeter of the room. There were more books on the desk and the bed – books everywhere.

As my eyes searched the room, not noticing anything remarkable, I began to feel both let down and amazed that one could just sit amongst all this clutter. As I turned in disappointment to leave the room, I saw it.

First one, and then others. Nasty magazines. Not *Playboy,* but sick, perverted images. I knew instantly. What I had intuitively known, seen, or overheard from my bedroom window years prior, that I was too young to grasp—that "dark thing" about my father was true.

I didn't know the details of it. The knowledge of it had been buried deep within my innocent mind. He had been doing something inappropriate from his bedroom towards the college girls living in the big house on the corner across from us.

I stumbled out of the room, locked the door, and ran into my room, slamming my door. My world had just cracked! Its shattered pieces were both inside me and lying on the floor all around.

I was shocked and sickened by my discovery. I had opened

Pandora's box and didn't know how to close it. I didn't know how to unsee what I had seen, didn't know how to turn off the deluge of thoughts and mixed feelings about my father. After all, one doesn't really want to admit that their father is a pervert.

Many years later, in my early twenties, I learned that he was an exhibitionist. He had indeed been exposing himself from his bedroom window to the college girls across the street.

Something Shriveled Up Inside of Me

"For everything that is hidden will eventually be brought into the open, and every secret will be brought to light." – Mark 4:22 NLT

In high school, and then later college, I pursued an interest in psychology and abnormal psychology. Perhaps I was trying to figure out how to hold the myriad of discoveries and situations relating to my family and myself which gripped my mind. The reality is that it is only now, so many decades later and with the assistance of an amazing spiritual director, that I have finally even begun to know how to fully hold my own fractured life with grace, let alone my Dad's. But thanks be to God, I am learning to embrace on an emotional level what I know to be true on an intellectual one, that we are each more than the most horrific thing we have done.

I read *The Shack* eons ago. However, it was the visual effect of the movie version, years later, that truly impacted me at my core. Watching the main character, Mack, in the judgment room with God, struggling to understand the deep layers that compose us, and coming to grips with the fact that only God knows all and can rightly judge, I finally got it.

Mack had been abused by his father. He had not forgiven him. Watching a scene of a little boy being treated horrifically, he was appalled and wanted to judge the perpetrator. The little boy in the scene was his father. His father became what he had survived and endured, yet not to such a severe degree with Mack.

It made me think about my own family system. I pondered not only the depth of what my father may have endured, but also tried to imagine his mother's pain.

I have two particularly fond memories of Grandma Grubbs. In the first, I am sitting on the back porch at her home as a young child, churning the ice cream maker. I could taste and feel the delicious flavor of the homemade ice cream on my tongue complementing her peach cobbler before it even reached my mouth.

The other is from times when I was in school at the University of Michigan in Ann Arbor where she lived. Sometimes I would come by her place for Sunday dinner; afterwards I would pull out her huge box of pictures. She would tell me stories about the past as we sorted through them.

There were some tales that she didn't share, though. Growing up, I was always confused whether Gwen was my cousin or my aunt. I must have overheard something that the grownups said in one of their conversations. It turns out that Grandma went into the hospital under her sister's name when she gave birth to Gwen. My great-aunt Eunice raised Gwen as her daughter. Apparently, all the grown folks knew.

Occasionally as a child, if one of us did something wrong, my mother would say, "That's that bad Taylor blood." If she was directing the comment to me, I would always reply, "I don't have any bad blood. I come from you. I have your blood."

I had no idea what the "bad Taylor blood" was a reference to. Even as a very young person, my spirit knew not to receive anything and everything spoken over me, at least prior to my armor being pierced.

Once, prior to a service at Brown-Hutcherson Ministries, where I was a minister-in-training, there was a conversation happening about one of the ministers who had recently experienced a stroke. I made some comments about a pain I had.

The pastor looked at me and said, "Your face is crooked and drooping. I think you may be having a stroke right now."

I immediately responded, "I rebuke that in the Name of Jesus. I am not having a stroke. By His stripes I am healed."

My face was not drooping or crooked. I merely had a slight pain on my left side.

Later, Denise, who was a friend at the time and a minister, chastised me for speaking that way to the pastor. I told her I couldn't just let the words he spoke over me stand. She didn't understand or agree. It didn't matter. When I am in my right mind and spirit, I don't accept everything that is erroneously decreed over me.

Grace

"For all have sinned and fall short of the glory of God; and all are justified freely by his grace through the redemption that came by Christ Jesus." – Romans 3:23-24 NIV

In my early 50s, while working on my Master of Arts degree as a Family Life Educator, one of the courses required us to complete a family genogram.

My eldest brother, Bruce, held most of the family history on both sides, so I reached out to him. Not only did he give me relatives' names, but he shared a fact that I had never previously heard: Grandma Grubbs' father, my great-grandfather Taylor, set their house on fire in Louisiana, ran off with another woman, and moved up north, eventually settling in Detroit.

I'm not sure how old Grandma was at the time, but she was still a child, not fully grown. Her mother and twin siblings were in the house. They died in the blaze. I don't know if her father knew that they were in there or not. I certainly would like to think that he didn't, that their deaths were accidental. Yet, it still begs the questions, "Why didn't you just run off and leave?" "Why did you need to set the house on fire?"

Recently, as I've been working on this book, Aunt Gwen shared that great-grandpa Taylor thought his wife had an affair with his brother. He didn't believe that the twins were his children. Even if he was right, who intentionally kills someone in a house fire? Obviously not a sane, rational person.

Great-grandfather Taylor is the source of that "bad blood" that my mother was referencing. I can't begin to fathom the impact of that tragedy on my grandmother. I learned later in life that she pretty much gave away my Aunt Ruth. She placed my father in a boys' boarding school for a time and apparently "lost" him once such that he ended up in an orphanage.

Yet, she took him out East the summers when she worked the hotels and/or resorts. Which is where he met my mother. She was 12 and he was 14. I also discovered that she was quite abusive towards my cousins, Aunt Ruth's children, and Gwen. I never saw that side of her.

They say that she feared my father and knew better than to mistreat Al's kids if she wanted to maintain any relationship with him. It was bad enough she had abused and neglected him; he would never allow it to happen to us.

The Shack reinforced the truth that we live in a broken, sinful world in which horrific things occur. Perhaps barring mental illness, I think it is only because things have been done to us, or left undone, that we become so flawed.

Most of my life folks have told me that I look like my mother, especially the older I get. She was stunning, so it's difficult for me to see it, but I suppose I do favor her in the later years.

One day, a man approached me with excitement. I was sitting in a restaurant. He said, "Your Al's daughter, aren't you? Albert McCreary."

I responded, "Yes."

He said, "I knew it the moment I saw you."

He went on to share that he had worked with my dad for years at Kelvinator. He never knew what happened to him. I shared that he had passed some years prior.

He told me what a good man my father was. How everyone appreciated his hard work with the union, representing them, fighting for their rights and fair pay. He said, "You know your dad would go out of his way to pick up the young guys who didn't have transportation, or give them a ride home. He would share wisdom and encourage them. He was a good guy."

My dad was a brilliant, loving man, who, considering his life story and the demons he battled, provided an incredibly stable home for us to grow up and thrive in. I share a small portion of his brokenness only because it impacted me and thwarted my development. I believe it also created an opening for demonic forces to come after me. Which they did.

IDYLLIC INCONGRUITY

"Do not say, "Why were the former days better than these?"
For it is not from wisdom that you ask this. Wisdom is as good
as an inheritance, an advantage to those who see the sun.
For the protection of wisdom is like the protection of money,
and the advantage of knowledge is that wisdom gives life
to the one who possesses it." – Ecclesiastes 7:10-12 ESV

The Normalcy of Childhood

"And so, I am sure confident that God, who began this
good work in you will carry it on until it is finished on
the Day of Christ Jesus." – Philippians 1:6 GNT

Idyllic incongruity, another oxymoron. That's the point – the peaceful, idealized rhythms of life are juxtaposed against the discordance, the lack of consistency and harmony. These pulses are both actively present and waning, like a wave that reaches a peak and then releases itself on the shore.

I daresay that I am not the only one whose childhood is reflective of this quandary. It is one of the reasons that I'm writing the book: the inappropriate inconsistencies hidden within many, if not all, of our "perfectly pleasant," normal lives.

Perhaps what you've read thus far has you thinking, *"Well, I'm not really sure your childhood was normal."* I get that. However, on a certain level, I do beg to differ. After all, rarely is anything a perfectly straight line. The gray area always exists. Nothing is either just black or white. Such is the normalcy of my childhood.

As a youngster, I watched *Andy Griffin, The Beverly Hillbillies,* and *The Flying Nun.* In that sense, I was part of dominant culture. I can remember paying a dollar to see the beach party movies at the theater with my girlfriends.

I can remember *Julia, The Cosby Show, Good Times,* and the emergence of other Black shows on TV with Black actors popping up. It was exciting and refreshing to see ourselves on the screen.

Going back to my early days, I remember attempting to nap next to the teacher's desk in kindergarten at Henry School, rarely sleeping, and her slipping me treats. As I've shared, we moved after kindergarten. I attended Alexander Elementary School in Grand Rapids, Michigan for first through sixth grades.

Mrs. Brink oversaw our school play and pageant every year. Students were generally not allowed to be in the program for consecutive years, but she always allowed me to participate whenever I wanted.

School was fun and easy. The teachers were mostly nice and helpful. The only times I found myself in trouble was following an assembly in which we were told not to walk in the streets and for fighting my next-door neighbor.

In my defense, the sidewalks were not shoveled, which is why some of us walked in the street. It was out of necessity, not disobedience. We had enough sense to watch out for cars.

Donald, my next-door neighbor, and I got into a fight one day. Mind you neither of us wanted to fight. However, the kids were egging him on, teasing him about being afraid of a girl, so he eventually hit me. Naturally, I had to defend myself. I ended up accidentally tearing his shirt.

Both incidents caused me to be sent home for the remainder of the day. Hmm? Do they think we mind being at home? Apparently. Wrong!

Daily Life

"As water reflects the face, so one's life reflects the heart." – Proverbs 27:19 NIV

I've shared that I grew up in a household of boys. The three oldest were seven, six, and four years my senior. They were my protectors and around for family trips, but not so much for day-to-day activities. By the time I was in high school, they were all off to college and beyond. The youngest one is five-and-a-half years behind me. We are closer now as adults than we were growing up.

My mother was an assistant buyer at Wurzburg's Department Store until they closed. Beginning in the fifth grade, through junior high school, I was allowed to help select some of my outfits. I always looked forward to going downtown at the end of summer and before Christmas to choose things that I liked.

Mom received a store discount, so nicer outfits were purchased there for the savings. Of course, all the sales ladies knew my mother. They were very friendly and helpful. They would hang my selections in their backroom to await my mother's approval or dismissal. I would excitedly await to discover which items made the cut!

Mom enrolled me in the charm school classes the store offered. I was taught how to sit properly with my legs crossed at my ankles. I walked around the house with a book on my head to ensure a straight posture. We learned how to set a proper table and the correct order of using the silverware and various dishes. At the end of our sessions, we participated in a grand fashion show, which opened the door to a few other modeling opportunities for me at the store.

My mother and I both had a penchant for the "girly" things while maintaining our practical, level-headed personas. Daddy took us all to the movies; but Mom and I went to see plays, musicals, and dances, and we also attended various church and social events together.

All of us were required to do chores on Saturdays and clean the house. Sometimes I could get out of it by accompanying my parents to the grocery store.

My eldest brother, Bruce, oversaw all of us on Saturdays. He couldn't take off with his friends until we finished our duties, so he was strict about us getting started and not being distracted watching cartoons. There was a comfortable consistency in the patterns and flow of life in those days.

School Days

"Train up a child in the way he should go; even when he is old he will not depart from it." – Proverbs 22:6 ESV

I had one set of friends at school that varied a bit from grade to grade. These were students that I got along with in class, perhaps sat besides, played with on the playground, and/or hung out with in the after-school programs. They didn't live in my immediate neighborhood, but we were school buddies.

As I noted previously, our neighborhood changed significantly from the time I attended first grade until I finished the sixth grade. Each year there would be more White families fleeing the area and new families of color moving in. This was true of my street and the two or three blocks adjacent to the corner that I lived on. There were always new kids to meet and the possibility of new friendships.

Our original next-door neighbors had moved the year after we arrived. Joanne's dad was hired to work at one of the auto plants in Detroit. At that time, they were the only other Black family on the block.

Shortly thereafter, the Greens, who were also Black, moved in next door. I played games outside with all of them every summer. Patty, the oldest girl, was a few years younger than me, so we didn't really hang out throughout the school year.

One summer, I hung out with Tina. Another summer, I was with Yolanda. One year I was around the corner at Dee's house.

Lynn's family moved in around the corner on Thomas Street around 4th or 5th grade. I liked the music that was always playing at their house, the freedom they seemed to have, and how mature they were. They knew things firsthand that I only knew from books and television.

The catch was that my mother had sort of forbidden me from being at Lynn's house or playing with her. She and her sister seemed not to have any parental supervision and knew things my mother didn't want me to know. My dad was a bit more lenient. I, of course, did go over to her house since I couldn't invite her to mine.

In 6th grade, I remember walking to and from school with Lynn, Dee, and Beverly. We came home for lunch back then. Towards the end of the second semester, they would all be over at Beverly's house during lunchtime. Dee forbade me to come over there. She told me that when it was time to walk back to school I needed to wait outside for Lynn and Beverly to come out. I felt excluded and resented this. But Dee could fight, so you didn't mess with her. She wouldn't tell me what was happening over the lunch hour, just that it wasn't for me. I didn't need to be a part of it.

Much later Dee shared that the two girls had been engaging

in sex with a couple of the boys during lunch hour. Already, in sixth grade! I was from what was considered a "good family" and innocent to things of that nature, so she protected me from being exposed to their lunchtime shenanigans.

Dee liked me. She not only looked out for me, but she spared me her wrath that was released upon the others. I don't know what they did to piss her off, but the last week of school Dee declared that she was going to beat up Lynn, along with a couple of other kids on the last day of class. She assured me that I was in the clear.

We were all hyped up, eager for the bell to ring so that we could run out of the building and see the fight. Sure enough, she was true to her word, clobbering the kids. I was so grateful that I wasn't part of the madness.

Many of the students at Alexander School lived in two different districts for junior high and high school. So, some of us ended up going our separate ways following that summer.

I tended to move on from one friend to the next without establishing deep roots throughout elementary school. This was primarily due to a difference of interests. I had a wider range of life experiences than many of the neighborhood kids since my parents took us to museums, events, and exhibitions, as well as on road trips, including traveling out East to visit my grandmother.

I was also a voracious reader. Daun was the first peer whom I met who also liked to read. Her parents were both educators so it came naturally for her.

I was grateful to meet her the first day of 7th grade as I was walking to school. We hit it off immediately. She had more friends than me, but in some ways was on the fringe, too.

We had a shared intellect, similar interests, and appreciated one another's sense of humor. We were just comfortable with one another! During the summer months we rode our bicycles all over the city, hung out at the Christian youth group down-town by St. Andrew's school, swam at the neighborhood pool, and enjoyed frequent sleepovers. We were "besties" throughout both junior high and high school. Our friendship didn't fade or wane until I went off to college.

Losing Things

"And I will restore to you the years that the locust hath eaten, the cankerworm, and the caterpillar, and the palmerworm…" – Joel 2:25 KJV

The summer after 6th grade, I went down to Alicia's house to play. She was a couple of years older than me and grooming me. Alas, I didn't know what that was at the time. I lost a sense of my value, worthiness, cleanliness, and self. All of which were replaced with feelings of guilt, shame, and dirtiness after being touched by my neighbor, my new playmate.

I questioned for years why I "allowed" it to happen to me. Why on earth did I go into the closet with her? Why did I let her pull my pants down? What could I have possibly been thinking? Why did I go back a second time and allow it to happen again?

Fifty some years later, I shared for the very first time what happened to me with another individual, my spiritual director. She suggested that it was a miracle that it only happened twice and gave me language for one of the things that resulted from it: I was sexualized early, sexually awakened.

I believe that this is one of the dark satanic strongholds on my father's side of the family. My father was molested as a child in boarding school and again later when he was placed to live for a time with a couple of guys who were predators. God only knows how many other times he may have been abused. I wouldn't be surprised if it happened when he landed in an orphanage for a period, as well.

There are others in the family whom I am sure have been

victimized and impacted over the course of the years. Those are their stories to tell.

Guilt and shame became constant companions of mine because of my unspoken secret and acts. The physical reality of being touched is that the sensation is a pleasant one. I began masturbating at a very early age. However, the spiritual, mental, and emotional reality is that I always felt dirty, less than, and condemned.

I came up in the age of the sexual revolution, the hippie movement, freedom of choice, and birth control, which also may have impacted me. Yet, I think my engagement in sexual relations in high school, rather than waiting until later in life, is probably directly correlated to this early violation and awakening.

FISSURES

THE SLIPPERY SLOPE

"Be very careful, then, how you live — not as unwise but as wise, making the most of every opportunity, because the days are evil." – Ephesians 5:15-16 NIV

Church Girl

"…but as for me and my household, we will serve the Lord." – Joshua 24:15 NRSV

Here's the thing: I grew up in the Episcopal Church from birth. For those of you not familiar with this denomination, the Episcopal form of worship is somewhat like the Catholic Church in its pageantry, but without the elevation, focus, and prayers to Virgin Mary. Episcopalians have bishops and cardinals, but no Pope. The priests are allowed to marry. They even have female priests now.

My father was agnostic. He only attended church events when my mother told him that he must escort her. His position regarding the children was that she could take us while we were young. Once we were old enough to decide for ourselves, she had to allow us to do so. I don't recall my brothers being at church

with us very often, but given our age differences, they had the
freedom to choose.

I wanted to go. I liked being at church with my mother. Our
small, mostly Black parish felt like family. We knew everyone.
I liked helping my mother set up and serve on our Sundays to
host the coffee hour following service.

Father Stephens was White, but he was cool! I was comfortable
talking to him. He was down to earth and patient, answering
our questions as we prepared for catechism. He was there until
I was in my teens and was my favorite of the two priests during
my attendance.

The steeple bell's melodic ring would welcome and beckon
us into church. On the High Holy Days, the incense could
be overdone, making it difficult to breathe, but I enjoyed the
spectacle of it all. The processional with the beautiful robes, the
acolyte carrying the Bible in front of the priest, the incense burner
swinging in concert with the music, and the somberness of it all
covered me in a mist of holiness and gave me peace.

The movements of the service were comforting to me. I
knew many of the prayers by heart, particularly the Prayer of
Humble Access.

"We do not presume to come to this your table, O merciful
Lord, trusting in our own righteousness, but in your manifold
and great mercies. We are not worthy so much as to gather up
the crumbs under your table; but you are the same Lord whose
property is to always grant mercy. Grant us, therefore, gracious
Lord, so to eat the flesh of your dear Son Jesus Christ, and to
drink his blood, that we may evermore dwell in him, and he in
us. Amen."

I knew what each color of the candles represented, so that I
could light the proper one as I lifted my prayer requests to God.

I've never questioned the reality of God; I've always known
that He is real. I can feel Him in music, hear or see Him in nature, and sometimes sense Him in people. I have always known

things intuitively, even as a small child. It's as if the knowledge of something is dropped or deposited into me. This has always been and is still true today. I've questioned, and still question, many things about God, the condition of the world, and certainly the state of the Church. But I've always known Him as Supreme Being and Creator.

All this to say that I grew up in a household where I was taught that sex outside of marriage is wrong. When I consciously decided to venture down to Planned Parenthood, I knew that had she known, my mother would be shocked and dismayed.

Crooked Feet

"For it was you who formed my inward parts; you knit me together in my mother's womb. I praise you, for I am fearfully and wonderfully made. Wonderful are your works; that I know very well. My frame was not hidden from you, when I was being made in secret, intricately woven in the depths of the earth." – Psalm 139:13-15 NRSV

I have shared bits of my story at women's conferences, playing off some of the language and images in the book *Hinds' Feet on High Places.* Hannah Hurnard's main character, Much-Afraid, is a cripple. Her feet are crooked, causing her to limp and stumble. Hurnard invites us into Much-Afraid's life and journey with the Great Shepherd as she learns how to overcome and walk on the high places.

Most of us are not born with actual crooked feet. Yet, many of us acquire them metaphorically. I acknowledge that at the beginning of our journeys, we are not aware of our feet becoming crooked due to the forces of life. Then there is a moment when eventually we do know. We begin to try to hide and mask our deformity.

I was a master at disguise.

No one could tell by looking at me that there was anything wrong. No one heard the loud noise when everything abruptly fell off the shelf and crashed. No one knew the deep-seated insecurities, the shame, or the void that had been created and was expanding.

The relationship with my first boyfriend started off in a relaxed, easy fashion. He was the best friend of my best friend's boyfriend. The four of us had been hanging out together all of the time since the 8th grade. It was a natural transition to make the relationship official during my sophomore year of high school.

Perry was attractive, funny, and easy-going. He often dressed like a Black Panther, with his black leather jacket and beret. Looking back, I'm not sure his interest and actions followed suit. Yet he appeared to be "good people" and seemed sincere in his feelings towards me.

It didn't take much persuasion to convince my best friend that we should go down to Planned Parenthood and secure birth control pills to have on hand just in case we might decide to start taking them.

That following summer, the four of us went on a picnic. Perry and I slipped off to a secluded spot in the park and had intercourse. I didn't really know what to expect, but I don't recall especially enjoying it.

We later engaged in the act once more before he stopped seeing me. No words were shared. No phone call, note, or message was sent via our mutual friends. When I called him, he refused to come to the phone. Nor would he come to the door when I went to his house. To say that I was devastated is an understatement. I didn't know how to process or hold that level of rejection, especially after having given away my virginity. It wasn't clear to me if he didn't enjoy me or if his perception of me had been diminished such that he just didn't want me. I felt like a worthless fool!

His rejection triggered the deep wound I had inside from my

father not always being present or showing love to me in the way that I needed to receive it.

Emotionally, I hurt terribly. I wanted him to hurt, too. I sent him a letter telling him that I was pregnant. I let him know that since he was a worthless good for nothing, I was going to have an abortion. No response. It was all a lie. I didn't know if it caused him any remorse or not. It certainly didn't prompt him to reach out to me.

I wasn't just heartbroken or embarrassed. I felt like a used, throw-away item. Dirty and damaged. I knew my "feet" were becoming gnarled and crooked.

Decades later, when I was around the age of 41 or 42, he called me out of the blue. He had run into someone who knew me and asked for my phone number. He had heard that I was walking with the Lord and doing well. Even though so many years had passed between us, he still desired to apologize. He wanted me to know that his rejection of me was a result of his fear.

The phone rings. "Hello."

"Hello, this is Perry."

"Oh my gosh! How on earth did you get my number? And, what has you calling me out of the blue after all these years?"

"I ran into someone who knows you. It made me think about you and those years when we were young. You know what happened between us has haunted me most of my life."

"I'm so sorry!"

"Yeah, I felt so bad just dropping you with no explanation. I wished that I hadn't let you go through that by yourself. The guilt and remorse were so heavy that I started drinking. I became an alcoholic which had a precarious impact on my life."

I wanted to hang up without saying anything. My careless lie had a devastating impact on his life that he didn't deserve. I felt miserable! I swallowed and gathered my courage.

"I have something difficult to say to you. I feel horrible. Not to make an excuse for it, but I didn't know how to hold your rejection at that young age. My immature response was to try and make you feel bad and guilty by telling you that I was pregnant. At that moment I was trying to get you to reach out to me. It was all a lie. I wasn't pregnant. I didn't have an abortion."

Silence.

"I feel so badly hearing how it disrupted your life for so many years. I had no idea. I am so truly sorry!"

I felt such heavy guilt wash over me, this time from lying and recklessly causing such a devastating impact on someone's life.

I said, "I totally understand if you are not able to forgive me. I had desired to hurt you because I was so deeply wounded. I didn't know that it led you to drink, or how it impacted your life."

I can't imagine what he thought upon hearing that. Or, how he felt. He was kind and gracious.

"I understand," he said. "We were so young and immature. We didn't know better. We didn't know the consequences of what we were doing."

I again asked for his forgiveness. "I pray for your peace, wholeness, and new life."

We said goodbye.

The messiness of immaturity, engaging in grownup acts that my youthful mind and emotions were unable to hold or process, had been foolhardy and life-shattering.

I thank God that we both had an opportunity to hear the truth. I pray that we were both set free, healed, and able to move on.

It was right before Christmas break during my junior year of high school that I met my next boyfriend. One of the girls thought that I liked a guy she had her eyes on, so she wrote something about me and Thomas on the Seniors' Christmas Wish List hanging in their hallway.

He sat down next to me during an assembly to check me, thinking I had written the note. "So, what's this about you being my best Christmas gift? I don't even know you. That's a bold move."

I laughed. "I would be a great gift if you were so lucky as to get me, but I didn't write that on the board. Janice did. She thought I was talking to Teddy, whom she is pursuing. She put that on the board so that he wouldn't take up an interest in me. He and I are just friendly classmates. I'm not interested in him, or you, since I don't even know you."

Thomas was a football player, accustomed to all the girls fawning over him; apparently, he found my aloofness and lack of interest attractive. We chatted throughout the assembly, and he asked if he might have my phone number. I gave it to him.

We hit it off right away. But he would come by my house early and leave early, as if I was stupid. I suggested that he not bother stopping by on the way to someone else's house. He corrected that behavior and we started going steady.

I was the square girl, not a part of any of the cool circles in high school. Folks were flabbergasted that we were a couple. He was shocked when he discovered that I wasn't a virgin. Sex with him was good. He was sweet, gentle, and kind; I could ask questions as we tried things together.

We did everything together. He took me out wherever I wanted to go. When my hours were cut at work, he would give me cash to make up the difference. His family adored me, and it was mutual.

My senior year, he came back to school to escort me to the big football game when I was voted onto the Homecoming Court.

We kept dating even after I started at the University of Michigan. My sophomore year, I stayed on a co-ed floor in the dormitory. Things were rocky between us by now. Thomas came down to visit, hoping to firm up our relationship. He stayed in my room. I can still remember him looking so cute in my long, blue, fluffy robe.

The girls on the floor, like girls everywhere, were enamored with him. They were furious and scolded me when they discovered that I had taken off in his car with Little Mike to go to the mall. "How could you do such a thing and treat him like that?" they asked.

"Easily," was my response.I still liked him, but had detached any deep feelings once I learned he wasn't the kind of guy who would be faithful. I dumped him at the end of that visit, following our conversation about me leaving with the car.

I believed he loved me, and if I had stayed with him, I am sure that he would have asked me to marry him. The kicker is that he wasn't faithful. Even before I went off to college, he was cheating on me. He would try to be clever and hide it, but I always knew.

We sat in his car and talked about everything before he left to head back home. "Tootsie Roll," I said, using his childhood nickname, "There's really no point in us saying that we are a couple while I'm here at school. You're doing your own thing at home. You always have cheated and hung out with other girls anyway."

"None of those girls ever meant anything to me. It was just sex. You know that. I've loved you from the moment we got together. You know how crazy I am about you," he replied.

"Yes, but you will never be honest and faithful. So why pretend that we're a couple, especially since I'm here at school most of the year?"

He profusely professed his love for me. I confess that I was surprised when he started crying while begging me to continue being his girlfriend. He proclaimed that I was the only one he truly cared about, not any of the others. I believed that was true, yet it wasn't enough.

Another failed relationship. Another promiscuous encounter. Another crook in my foot!

I knew Thomas was unfaithful, and so the year before that happened, to "get even" the summer after my freshman year at college, I had a fling with one of the guys from high school – Teddy, the same guy Janice had been trying to keep me from my junior year in high school. He and I had always been cool, just friends, nothing more. Since Thomas was going out of town with the guys chasing girls and I kept catching him ducking and dodging me in town with one girl, I decided to fool around, too. I would show him!

I was only with Teddy one time. I got pregnant. I couldn't believe my "bad luck." I knew that I wasn't prepared to be a parent at the age of 19. Once the pregnancy was confirmed at Planned Parenthood, I scheduled an appointment to have an abortion before I returned to school.

My mother had a gift, or a curse, depending upon how you looked at it. She, too, knew things. More than that, she saw things. I can't recall anything that she ever saw and shared with me that didn't happen.

The only exception is her seeing me in a big, expensive home with my husband. I don't have either one. At least not yet—and I'm not getting any younger.

At any rate, I was running the water to soak in the bathtub after my procedure. Mom came upstairs and softly said, "If you just did what I think you did you shouldn't soak in the tub."

I replied, "I don't know what you're talking about."

She answered, "Your body is open to germs and infections right now. It's too soon for you to take a bath." I responded once again that I didn't know what she was talking about, filled the tub, and got in.

I couldn't confess that I was a whore and a murderer to anyone beyond myself. Certainly not my mother! Thankfully, the bath didn't harm me. No, it was my lifestyle and actions that did that.

When we're naïve and innocent, and folks pick us up and use us like we have no value, we often come to believe that we don't. Certainly, this is true on an unconscious level, if not a conscious one.

And, if there was any essence of morals in your home, or church life, it can compound you seeing yourself as being unclean and worthless. Shame and guilt start hanging out with you.

It isn't long before they become constant companions—always lurking about in the background, sometimes boldly creeping up into the forefront. This became my daily reality.

THE WORLD TURNED
UPSIDE DOWN

"When Gideon came, behold, a man was relating a dream to his friend. And he said, "Behold, I had a dream; a loaf of barley bread was tumbling into the camp of Midian, and it came to the tent and struck it so that it fell, and turned it upside down so that the tent lay flat." – Judges 7:13 NASB

Compartments

"Make for yourself an ark of gopher wood; you shall make the ark with compartments, and cover it inside and out with pitch." – Genesis 6:14 NASB

I was in my late 20s when I started working at Blue Cross and Blue Shield of Michigan. One of my co-workers and I struck up somewhat of a friendship outside of work. She had multiple personality disorder, or what is called dissociative identity disorder these days. She had numerous, splintered personalities living within her because of the severe trauma she endured, beginning as a very young child.

Each of the personalities liked and, more importantly, trusted me; so, they eventually popped out, introducing themselves. They included other women and children of various ages and genders. It was fascinating to witness the metamorphosis! Their voices and mannerisms were remarkably distinct. The breaks seemed to have occurred at various stress points during childhood, resulting in each of them having specific personality traits, skill sets, and areas of focus.

The brain's ability to hold memories, interpret and process data, compartmentalize, stabilize emotions, and handle our daily living functions is nothing short of a miraculous wonder.

I thank God that I wasn't traumatized to the extent that my mind totally broke off into fragmented personalities, but it clearly did categorize and file memories and emotions so that I could function in a relatively normal fashion.

I was a mature, adept, professional and/or student who easily excelled at work or college. Yet, I was insecure and non-trusting in relationships with guys. I would typically be either aloof and not caring, or clingy and desperately wanting someone to love and cherish me, which never happened.

As I've previously noted, very few other folks saw my "crooked feet." I looked and, for the most part, functioned normally on a day-to-day basis, particularly in the public arena. Yet, inside I was emotionally shrinking and shriveling like a plant quenched for water.

How Do You Choose?

"Show me your ways, LORD, teach me your paths." – Psalms 25:4 NIV

I marveled at the people I knew growing up who seemingly had a sense of self from birth. They came into the world knowing who they were and explored their interests and talents. As early as elementary or junior high, they knew what course they wanted their lives to take, and what they wanted to be when they grew up. They were focused with intentionality, and made choices to move in that direction.

I never had that. I didn't have a clue what I might want to do as an adult. There wasn't any one thing that captured my interest, or that I felt particularly skilled or gifted at. Quite the contrary, things that were easy for me I took for granted. Although my entire life I desired to be special, I didn't see myself as such. I certainly didn't have a specific talent. I was clueless as to what to do with myself.

In high school, it was automatic that the classes I took were the mandatory ones for college entrance—though I had zero interest in going to college. *Why would anyone enroll in college if you didn't know what career you wanted to pursue?* I wondered. The school counselors failed to share any helpful insights beyond their proclamation that I could do anything I wanted based upon my personality, grades, and test scores. Therefore, all I had to do was select something.

Excuse me! That's the point. I don't know what to select. I thought they were paying you to assist us in the process, not merely tell me my test scores and aptitude were high. Tell me something I don't already know that is beneficial! Then—wonder of wonders! Miraculously, an intriguing invitation presented itself.

Senior year, I joined the debutante circle in preparation for coming out in the spring Cotillion. This has a long history in Black culture following being freed from slavery. Many who acquired middle-to-upper-middle class status by holding professions such as teaching, medicine, or law had their daughters participate as debutantes in hopes of meeting a young man from a suitable family.

Over the years, it shifted more to a focus of preparing the

young women and men to think about college and the professional avenues they might pursue.

One part of the debutante process was attending classes and field trips. Our big excursion was a trip to Chicago to tour several Black-owned businesses, which was a big deal back in the early 1970s. I remember the outfit I was wearing that day: a small, diagonal-checkered red and white suit. The top jacket was form-fitting with single buttons down the front. The pants had a slight bit of flare at the bottom. I had a red turban on my head.

I was walking up front with our tour guide as we meandered through Johnson Publishing. She was pointing out items of interest to the group even as she and I had a private conversation going on. As we neared the end of our tour, she began talking about the Ebony Fashion Fair that was held all around the country. She noted that I would fit right in as a model. I was flabbergasted! Me? Really? Wow! She introduced me to someone in that area who conducted a short interview and gave me a packet of information with instructions on what I needed to do to begin with the group in the fall.

I was on cloud nine! There was only one slight stipulation. The models had to report in August, and must be 18 years of age at that time. I will turn 18 that September. They liked me, so they said if I had parental permission for the first month, they would waive the age requirement since my birthday was so close to the starting date.

I couldn't wait to share the news with my mother. Before I share her response, let me disclose this: I had taken the SAT prior to the Chicago trip. I don't recall my score, but I tested in the top 2% nationally. I had brochures coming in the mail from colleges and universities all around the country. Mind you, I had no interest in going to college.

At some point, my father inquired where I had applied to go to school; I informed him that I hadn't. He instructed me to do so at once, so I begrudgingly obeyed by applying to one. He later asked again who I had sent applications to, and I told him the University of Michigan. He asked, "Where else?" to which I replied, "Nowhere. I can only go to one school."

"Well, what if they don't accept you?"

I didn't respond, but my thought was... *Well now, isn't that ludicrous. Why wouldn't they?* I said, "Ok, I'll send an application to Michigan State University." I wanted to raise my voice with inflection and say, *"Now will you leave me alone, already."*

I received my acceptance letter from MSU first. Weeks later, the letter came from U of M. I also had a scholarship and full funding, including incidental monies for each semester.

Back to the offer to model with Ebony Fashion Fair. I excitedly shared with mom everything that happened in Chicago. She politely listened and then responded, "Well, you know you will have to ask your father."

"DADDY!"

"Yes, Deb-Deb, what is it? What are you yelling about?" I shared my news about the Ebony Fashion Fair with him. He, too, politely, quietly listened, not interrupting, allowing me to get it all out. But he was looking at me as if I had a screw loose.

Once I finished, he matter-of-factly, softly stated, "You have a full scholarship to the University of Michigan. That's where you are going in the fall. Your mother and I will not be signing anything granting our permission for you to do otherwise."

I was livid!

Dad had gone to the University of Michigan after serving in World War II. He was expelled for correcting a White professor in front of the class, refusing to back down, and not apologizing. Mom attended Hunter College in New York until she married him and moved to Michigan. My eldest brother Bruce attended Hope College. Steve and Albert Jr. went to U of M and David attended Western Michigan University.

It was an unspoken, understood standard that the next step following high school was college. The fact that I had no desire or vision for attending a university was irrelevant to him. My course was set.

Little did he, or I, know how, or why it would abruptly end, only to be completed many years later.

Beginning College Years

"To everything there is a season." – Ecclesiastes 3:1a NKJV

I selectively attended the initial session of our freshman orientation on campus at the University of Michigan. I did not show up and participate in any of the testing they scheduled for us. They determined some of my class placement levels based upon my high school transcripts and my SAT scores.

The second day of orientation, Robin, my roommate from Grand Rapids, and I ran into a few guys as we were crossing the Diag on Central Campus. We jumped into the car with them and hung out, getting high.

Jake was in law school. He became a friend and like a big brother to me. Others implied he was interested in more, but he had a girlfriend in Washington D.C. whom I had met. I respected their relationship. Nor was I attracted to him in that way. To make that point clear, I hung out with his friend, Chet, for a bit once I convinced him that Jake would get over it.

Anyway, their spot became my hangout during my first semester on campus. So much so that when I began hanging out in my dorm after Thanksgiving break, some of the girls on my floor thought I was a new student.

Jake's girlfriend came up from D.C. to visit one weekend. I was there cooking for everyone. Jake and the boys were selling marijuana. I was totally unaware that they were also using angel dust. I started walking from the kitchen towards the living room carrying a plate of food in each hand. Suddenly something hit me! I dropped everything as I began to fall. Jake rushed to catch me. He began yelling at the other guys, asking what they had given me. They said, "Nothing. She rolled a joint. She must have used the wrong batch of weed."

I had inadvertently smoked some of the marijuana laced with angel dust. Jake was furious! He carried me upstairs and laid me on the bed. They got cold compresses for me and a glass of water. The guys did shifts sitting bedside to make sure that I was going to be okay. My body was still and resting, but my mind was racing with multitudes of images. I couldn't make it slow down or stop. I was there for hours before they felt it was safe to take me back to my dorm.

It scared me. I knew that I would never experiment with strong drugs. My visits to the guys' spot became less frequent.

Towards the end of my freshman year, Jake jumped off the top of my dormitory building. He had a vision that if he survived, God was going to give the world more time to get our act together. If he died, the world was coming to an end. He fractured his wrist and ankles.

His boys were upset with me when I came to the hospital to visit him. They blamed me for the jump. "What are you doing here? You know Jake became unglued because you rejected him."

I responded, "That's B.S. and you know it. First, I didn't reject him. We're cool. We're good friends. And, secondly, he became undone because of all the PCP he was using. He had a bad trip hallucinating."

Once Jake came around, he told me not to listen to the guys. It was totally his fault. He had a bad reaction to the angel dust. His parents came up from Washington D.C., and upon his release from the hospital, they took him home. I have wondered over the years what became of him. He had such a quick, brilliant mind. He would be an amazing attorney.

I attended my elective classes of interest. I disregarded the second level French class I was assigned to. I had dropped out of my fourth year of high school French because, although I could read and understand it, I wasn't proficient at speaking it. I couldn't roll my r's. I didn't know that the college language requirement could be waived with four years of a high school language, but it wouldn't have mattered at the time if I had known.

I finally got called on the carpet about not attending the French class. I explained that I had been under unexpected pressure due to my present family situation. My manic-depressive father was having one of his episodes. He was currently across the way from my North Campus dormitory in the V.A. psychiatric unit, requesting visits with me.

I went to visit him once or twice. The thought of him, his mental condition, and wondering if he had day passes and might show up at the dorm annoyed me. I was furious that he had decided to come to the V.A. hospital in Ann Arbor rather than going to the one in Battle Creek. In retrospect, I don't know if that was his choice or where they placed him based upon open space.

I was stressed, but promised to turn things around. They placed me on academic probation for the remainder of the semester. I dropped the two classes I wasn't attending and received an A in all the others. School life went on.

Seeking Care, Safety, Shelter, or Something

"He will cover you with his feathers and under his wings you will find refuge; his faithfulness will be your shield and rampart." – Psalm 91:4 NIV

I don't know when my father first began receiving psychiatric treatment for his various disorders. I do recall my mother mentioning that they experimented and did different behavior modification treatments on him when they lived in Ann Arbor, presumably while he was enrolled at the University.

I don't know if they curbed his behaviors or not; they did not eliminate them. He was prescribed various psychotropic drugs over the years. Since he did not take them regularly—either because of the unwanted effects of the drugs or because he preferred the manic high at times—positive impact was seemingly insignificant, or at least inconsistent.

He was periodically in and out of various psychiatric hospitals. I visited him at the V.A. Hospital in Battle Creek as a child, in addition to their facility in Ann Arbor when I was at the University. I also recall him being at Forest View here in Grand Rapids.

I remember taking him a carton of cigarettes when he was at Kent Oaks Psychiatric Hospital in Grand Rapids. The attendant was so pleased that one of Al's family members had come to see him. Dad had fabricated this woven tale of that being his first time down and out. The family didn't know how to process it and had abandoned him. The guy was so glad that I was coming around. I laughed and told him the truth about dad being in and out of hospitals my entire life. My mother and I always visited him. I used to wonder just what tales Daddy did tell the various doctors and staff personnel since he was much smarter than most of them even with his mental illness.

WHAT JUST HAPPENED

MORE THAN MEETS THE EYE

"For if they fall, one will lift up his fellow. But woe to him who is alone when he falls and has not another to lift him up." – Ecclesiastes 4:10 ESV

Not Believing, Accepting, or Knowing How to Hold Truths

"Then you will experience for yourselves the truth, and the truth will free you." – John 8:32 MSG

It happened during winter break of my junior year of high school. David was home for Christmas on break from Western Michigan University. His friends came by that evening to pick him up and head back down to Kalamazoo, but David was sleeping and wouldn't wake up. He didn't wake up until mid-morning the next day.

I was in the kitchen. We had a big, bright, sunny kitchen. I had painted it a mild, mellow yellow one summer. I didn't realize what a big job I had taken on, so Dad helped me out by painting the large pantry. It was a warm, welcoming space to cook and sit, lingering over a meal.

David came downstairs and it was obvious that something was off. He seemed a bit out of it, unsteady on his feet. He sat down at the table with a distant, vacant stare, as if he was somewhere else.

"Are you hungry?" I asked him.

"Yes, do you mind cooking me some bacon and eggs? You know how to keep the bacon straight."

"Of course. I don't mind."

He always said he couldn't get the bacon to come out as straight and crisp as I could, his go-to method of persuasion whenever he wanted me to cook breakfast. It usually worked. It wasn't needed that morning because I knew that something was askew.

"You missed your ride last night," I shared, as he slowly ate. I took a deep breath as I gathered my courage. "What's going on? What's wrong? Aren't you going back to school?"

"No. I'm not going back to school. I tried to kill myself last night. I don't understand why I'm still here. Why I woke up."

I couldn't grasp why on earth he would do such a thing, yet I knew he was telling the truth.

"How?"

"I took a bottle of pills," he responded. "Promise me that you won't tell Mom. You know it will really upset her. Promise."

I adored David. "I promise." It all was stated so matter of fact; it was surreal. It was as if he had just told me he fell and scraped his knee, rather than sharing something so life-shattering. I promised that I wouldn't tell Mom even as I began trying to figure out what to do so that I could honor the promise but also get help.

I ended up calling Aunt Edna at work. She was mom's best friend, made of steel, and able to handle any situation. I told her what was going on, and she told me to bring Mom down to the hospital where she worked. "Tell her it's an emergency," she said.

Aunt Edna shared what had happened with my mother. They called Project Rehab, a drug rehabilitative program, whose operation just happened to be in a huge house at the end of our block. The guy came by and examined my brother and spoke with him. He told us that the drugs David had taken the day before had cleared his system by now, so he was out of any immediate physical danger. He recommended that David schedule an appointment with a therapist and begin counseling. But David never did participate in any counseling.

I'm not sure how Mom processed all of this. We did talk about it, on and off, over the years. She shared her pain, and her frustration not knowing how to help her child. As a mother myself now, I can't fully comprehend how she held such pain, terror, grief, sadness, disappointment, and loss with such strength.

I certainly didn't know what to make of it at age 16. My brother was beautiful, gifted, and smart, with the whole world open before him. Why on earth did he want to die? He didn't go back to school. He worked for the city one summer, and then for the railroad for a short stint until he suffered a minor injury.

Following his suicide attempt, we would meet in his bedroom, sitting on the lower bunk beds across from one another. We would engage in our mini-sessions. I was taking a psychology class and thinking of possibly pursuing that, so we practiced.

He talked about the girl he liked ending up with one of his closest friends. He told me that he was a heroin addict. I didn't believe him. I knew he smoked weed. I had taken some from his stash at one point as payback for him violating my trust and reading my diary in 9th grade. I knew at some point I would want to try it so I put it away for that day.

"There's no way you're doing that. You're not shooting up heroin! Let me see your arms. There aren't any tracks on them."

He laughed. "I would never do anything so obvious. I shoot up between my toes."

I had never heard of such a thing. I certainly didn't believe it. But I didn't ask to see his toes, either. I don't recall how many times we sat in his bedroom talking, but I do remember how it calmed my nerves. Each time, I convinced myself that whatever was troubling him would work itself out. He was going to be alright. He had to be.

In retrospect, I don't think I ever believed his story of being an addict because he didn't fit the image I had of addicts from TV, movies, and books. Or, perhaps, I couldn't believe it just because he was my brother.

My innocent delusion was shattered my first summer back home from U of M when I attended a party at someone's home. I walked up the steps, crossed the wide porch, and entered the huge living room where the party was being held.

The first thing I saw was David slouched over in a chair in a deep nod. He looked just like a junkie in a movie. The scene seemed like a slow-motion movie. Music was playing. Everyone that was dancing and standing around talking appeared to be in the background. The camera shot was tight on David, bringing him to the forefront with the spotlight directly on him.

My heart crashed to the floor. My head filled up with tears that felt like they would begin to leak and then gush from every orifice. I was fighting to hold them back.

My mind and emotions were racing, swirling; first shock, then sadness, then anger towards him, and rage that his friends allowed him to sit in the middle of the room so exposed. All of this occurred in the sixty seconds it took me to dash from the house and stumble into my car before letting the tears flow. I began trying to pick up the pieces of my heart so that I could drive home.

At some point, David showed me his sawed-off shotgun and the places he kept it—in the basement or the big, black crate in the attic. He told me stories of gang escapades that I had trouble believing, again, because I didn't want to.

A decade later, I was high on cocaine and intoxicated at a jazz spot following a management meeting at the Blue Cross Blue Shield of Michigan headquarters in Detroit. I saw a nice-looking guy sitting across the room. Later, I glanced and he was gone. I thought, *"I know you. You'll return before I leave."* Sure enough, he did.

I picked up my drink, went across the room, and sat down next to him at the bar. "I know you. You're a boxer." He denied it. He said he was a wealthy businessman, a mover and shaker. "Well, you used to box. You came to my house one weekend and stayed while you were preparing for a fight. I remember, you went to the YMCA to work out, and lose some weight, or bulk up, or something. I remember. I was in 9th or 10th grade. I thought you were so handsome. You had a ponytail."

Smiling with bewilderment, he responded, "You're David's little sister."

"Yes, I am."

We sat there talking for a while. He commented, "You listen to music with your whole body, the same way he did."

He shared numerous memories of his and David's time at WMU. "You know it was our good friend Conrad who got David addicted to heroin. Conrad started using it while he was serving in Vietnam. He was an addict when he came home from the war." Derek had been holding this against Conrad for years.

"That may be true about Conrad being an addict, but it wasn't his fault that David chose to use the drug. David was battling personal demons. The heroin probably helped him keep them at bay," I said. "It's time for you to let go. You need to forgive Conrad and reconcile with him. David would want you to do that."

"How on earth did you recognize me after all these years?" he asked. I responded, "Things just come to me. I saw you sitting across the room earlier and I just knew."

He thanked me. God used me to bless him even though I was such a mess myself, because God is like that.

David attempted suicide a second time during my freshman year at Michigan. He had checked into a hotel and then called a friend to let them know where he was, presumably, so they could later recover his body.

My mother said that the police responded to the friend's phone call, but David played it off as a prank. They left. His friend came by the hotel just to be sure that David was ok. He convinced the hotel manager to unlock the door when David didn't respond to his banging. They found him in bed unconscious and called for an ambulance. He was rushed to the hospital. When he woke up and realized that he was still alive, he tried to jump out of the hospital window.

He was serious about ending his life. Twice now he should have died based upon what he had ingested. I guess God wasn't ready to release him. David always said that the next time he would use a gun.

He's Gone

"And the dust returns to the earth as it was, and the spirit returns to God who gave it." – Ecclesiastes 12:7 ESV

He came up missing my sophomore year at Michigan. His personal items were left on the desk in his bedroom. Given his history, my folks wondered about another suicide attempt. They asked his friends if they had seen him. They tried to look for him, but how do you really do that?

He was gone for weeks. I came home in March for spring break, and that Friday evening dad and I were talking about David. The shotgun came up in our conversation. I said, "I know where he keeps it." I looked in the basement, but it wasn't there. I checked the big, black crate in the attic. Not there, either.

The next morning, daddy went to pick up some Valium to calm mom's nerves. I was upstairs in my bedroom. Mom was downstairs in the basement putting a load of clothes in the washer. Suddenly, I heard her scream. She came dashing up the stairs.

I said to myself, *"She's seen him in a vision. He's in the house."* She ran up the flights of stairs, into his bedroom, threw open the attic door, and screamed again. He was lying next to the big, black crate that I had looked in the previous evening. The sawed-off shotgun was next to him.

He had been there in the attic for weeks. March was cold that year. There was no smell of the body in the house. More importantly, God didn't let me see him next to that box.

I spent spring break attending his memorial service. The day of the funeral was total déjà vu; I had previously seen and heard everything that occurred that day. I knew what we were going to do next – what people were going to say. I had seen the silver casket - the orange and yellow flowers and the ribbon streamers. It was exactly as I had seen it, the only variance being the addition of his name on the ribbon.

I returned to school that weekend. My dorm mate, Robin, had moved out during the first semester after getting pregnant and then married.

I was all alone, secluded in the room with the memory of what had just happened. I experienced night terrors, and had dreams of death. I was screaming at the top of my lungs so loudly that I woke up the folks on my dorm floor. The residential advisor had to unlock my door two or three times to wake me up.

"You know we can't keep doing this. You won't be able to stay in the dorm if you continue in this state. I understand what you just went through, but the screaming in the middle of the night is just too disruptive. Isn't there someone who could stay with you?" she suggested. "Possibly that might help you sleep through the night."

It did. Little Mike spent the night with me for a few weeks, and the night terrors went away. I stopped screaming. I met with my professors, told them why I had been absent for a couple weeks, made up all of my work, and successfully finished the semester.

I also got pregnant again. I had another abortion. I came home for the summer having decided that I would not be returning to school in the fall.

I felt guilt and remorse about the abortion, but I could put that in a compartment. There wasn't a space large enough inside of me to hold the loss of my brother. It was as if the world had crashed, even though I had known it was merely a matter of time before he was successful in his attempt to end his life. I couldn't fathom someone I loved blowing their brains out. I didn't know how to hold the pain of his death. It was as if nothing made sense and there was no purpose to life.

Towards the end of the summer, Aunt Ruth, my favorite aunt, died from cancer. I told my parents I couldn't handle going to her funeral so close after my brother's. They went down to Ann Arbor for the service without me.

I moved into my own furnished apartment while they were gone without having given them any advance notice. I didn't want to see them. I didn't want to be around anyone unless it was required ... like the people I worked with who didn't really know me.

MINDLESSNESS

EARLY ADULT YEARS

"So that we may no longer be children, tossed to and fro by the waves and carried about by every wind of doctrine, by human cunning, by craftiness in deceitful schemes." – Ephesians 4:14 ESV

It's a Process

"When I was a child, I spoke like a child, I thought like a child, I reasoned like a child. When I became a man, I gave up childish ways." – 1 Corinthians 13:11 ESV

I once worked for a residential treatment facility with youth. After a while, I was let go. Ironically, it was not for the time I was on an outing with some of the youth and damaged our vehicle after smoking part of a joint on the way to work. I don't know if that contributed to the incident or not, because I'm not always aware of my surroundings, and I'm also a bit of a klutz.

I didn't notice the concrete parking block in front of the car and drove the car forward over it. The car wasn't stuck, but I didn't know how much additional damage I would do either driving forward over it or reversing. I called a staff person back at the residents' cottage and told them we needed help. Oddly, not much of a fuss was made about the incident.

The reasons stated for my dismissal were my refusal to eat the dinner served to the kids one night and causing Howard to miss his designated bedtime a few evenings. The real reason was because I challenged their treatment of the youth and their policies. Or, that I was a female person of color who should have shown gratitude for my position rather than questioning authority.

Howard was Black, and they were housing him at the facility in Lowell, a town outside of Grand Rapids (which at that time was a very bigoted, racist community). It may still be; I wouldn't be at all surprised. He was the only person of color at school and was bullied daily. They could have placed Howard at the house on Wealthy Street in Grand Rapids proper which would have been a much more accepting and comfortable placement for him, but they didn't.

Once our chores and assignments were completed, I would sit on a chair with Howard seated on the floor between my legs. I would oil his scalp and braid his hair. It was a time for him to exhale—a time to feel loved, valued, and cared for. A time to be reminded that he mattered.

Many years later, during a period when I needed a boost, I happened to encounter Howard walking down the street. He was a handsome young man. He approached me and asked if I knew who he was. I looked for a moment into his eyes, smiled, and said, "Howard," as I reached out to hug him.

He told me how significant that small act of braiding his hair had been, how it had anchored him so that he could endure and move forward. He let me know that he was doing well. I thanked God for the timing of the encounter, for meeting my need for encouragement by letting me know that He had used me to make a difference.

Seemingly Random Work

*"May the favor of the Lord our God rest on us;
establish the work of our hands for us – yes, establish
the work of our hands."– Psalm 90:17 NIV*

I had so many different jobs during my early twenties that it's impossible to remember the order. I worked at various department stores: Jacobson's Montgomery Wards, Hudson's, and Marshall Fields.

During the summer of 1975, when I moved into my own place, I began working at Transamerica Insurance Company. I remember feeling very confident when I interviewed for the position. Bob, the office manager, said I would hear back by that Friday. I didn't, so I called him. I guess he was on the fence about it, but he eventually called back and offered me the position.

Our small office was located on the top floor of an old, historic building. I loved the architecture! There was a warm, homey feeling to the space.

In addition to Bob, there was a female receptionist and four claims adjusters, one of whom was a woman. Betty took me under her wing and trained me. The guys were friendly and encouraging. Everyone was nice. It was the first time they had worked alongside a person of color, but I felt genuinely accepted.

One of my favorite memories is the year we did the Progressive Dinner. It was my first time experiencing this. You move from house to house for the various courses. We stopped at one house for appetizers and cocktails. We made another stop for soup and salad. My mother hosted the main meal at our home. We finished off with desserts at someone else's place. It was great! Such fun!

I enjoyed learning the business. It was a good opportunity. There was a genuine respect of one another and a spirit of camaraderie that I hadn't previously experienced in the workplace.

Perhaps a year or so into the job, I heard of another company with seemingly more growth opportunities that offered a greater salary. I applied and was offered the position. When I told Bob, he asked me why I wanted to make the change. When I told him the ways I would be able to grow, he promised me expansions in my position – new opportunities that would surpass what the other place was offering. He then said, "I won't offer you a pay increase though, that shouldn't be the basis of your decision." I think he understood my desire to pursue more money, but he was certainly disappointed when I gave my notice. He had been a great supervisor and mentor!

They say hindsight is 20-20 vision. I later regretted that decision and often wondered in what ways things might have been different in my life if I had remained at the company. In retrospect, it may have been an atmosphere conducive to emotional healing for me.

That's a lesson I've always remembered. Salary should never be the ultimate determining factor for a position. The people, the relationships, mutual respect, the atmosphere, and the opportunities for growth are significantly more important than the salary—especially when the dollar amounts are relatively close. I learned this lesson the hard way, declining Bob's offer and taking the new position.

I didn't like the people as well, nor all of the company politics and rules. I ended up leaving with no notice when they refused a vacation request. That is, I went on vacation, returned, and found a new job.

I always worked, generally steadily, with an increase in pay as I moved about. Sometimes I would work two jobs. The motions of life at this time were work and play, hanging out with girlfriends or a random guy here and there. Nothing serious.

I had no vision for my life. That didn't exist even prior to David taking his own life, and it certainly was non-existent at this stage.

My brother's suicide left me feeling disconnected from God, and thus everything else. It was as if I was floating through the world, unattached; I was without a mooring. There wasn't anything significant to ground me. I didn't care about myself, my own existence—so how could I care about anyone or anything else?

Random Choices

"The heart of the discerning acquires knowledge, for the ears of the wise seek it out." – Proverbs 18:15 NIV

I lived in two different apartments after dropping out of school, but living on my own didn't last that long. I was living at home when I was hanging out with JT, the guy I mentioned at the very beginning of this tale.

He didn't stay in Portland; he moved back, and we started talking again. But he quickly began to get on my nerves. We weren't a couple—it wasn't supposed to be serious. He was becoming too clingy.

I tried to let him down easily. "I think we should stop hanging out together. It feels like our interests have shifted. We might just want to go our separate ways," I told him.

He responded, "No, it's cool, we'll just be friends."

I said, "That's all we have ever been! We're not a couple. It feels like you're trying to be possessive in ways that aren't alright with me." He said that he wasn't aware of it and promised to stop. You can see where this is going, can't you?

I came home from hanging out at the club with my girlfriends one Friday night. JT pulled up in the driveway behind my car before I could even close the garage door.

An alarm bell should have gone off in my head at this strange behavior, but unfortunately, I realized this after the fact. He asked me to get in the car for a moment to talk, and thinking nothing of it, I did. He took off driving around the city, fussing at me.

By the time we were on the highway, he was quite agitated. He grabbed a handful of my hair and held it tightly while he slammed my head against the window whenever he felt a need to punctuate something he was saying. The frequency of hits against the glass pane increased as he worked himself more and more into a frantic craze.

I began evaluating the probability – whether I could jump out of a car moving at 70+ mph without significant injury compared to the injury my head was receiving every time it knocked against the glass. I remained in the car.

He eventually took me to his parent's home, where he lived. He had fashioned an apartment down in the basement with a couch, coffee table, and television. He had a space cordoned off as his bedroom with a full-size bed and dresser.

He held my arm firmly as he took me over to the bed. His expression was blank. His voice was cold and emotionless when he spoke. "Take your clothes off and lay on the bed." I did. I was praying and thinking, *Do whatever you're going to do, just let me get out of here alive in one piece.*

Then, suddenly, without touching me, he said, "Get up. Put your clothes back on." I was crying softly and my hands were shaking as I reached for my clothes and clumsily dressed. He seemed embarrassed and sheepish. In a soft voice he said, "Come on. I'll take you home."

He called the next day. "I don't know what got into me last night. I apologize. I am so sorry! I didn't mean to treat you that way."

"I survived," I responded. "I haven't told anyone. Apology accepted, so that's the end of that. We'll just go our separate ways. Please don't call again. I won't be seeing you anymore."

I could feel him holding back his anger through the phone as he spoke. "I said I was sorry. It won't happen again. I want us to be friends."

"That is now impossible. You take care. Goodbye."

I didn't tell a soul. I felt like a fool. How dare he bang my head and threaten to rape me! I was too embarrassed to speak up and resolved that I would suffer quietly. The lesson was learned. Never again. My mother knew something was wrong, but she didn't press me.

That Monday, JT arrived at my place of employment. He was very calm as he politely insisted that I give him just a few minutes to talk with me. I didn't want him to create a scene, so I allowed him into the conference room.

"Look, I accept your apology, but I need you not to call me or come by my house any more. I can't believe that you would come to my job for this conversation. This is totally out of order! It's embarrassing and puts my job in jeopardy." I stated kindly but emphatically that our friendship had run its course.

He began yelling at me. "I apologized. I'm trying to make up and you're just going to diss me? It's not happening. I am sorry. And, I want to keep seeing you." At this point he began chasing me around the conference table. I was knocking over chairs to slow him down and keep myself out of his reach. "You think you're special, don't you? You ungrateful bitch."

Ron, the office manager, came storming into the conference room demanding that JT leave immediately. There were a few other guys just outside of the door for backup. Ron advised that he had called the police, and JT left.

Ron asked what was going on. I told him a bit of what had happened that weekend. "Did you notify the police?"

"No," I responded. "I just wanted it to be over and done." He told me to leave and go down to the police station.

"Tell them everything that happened on Friday and what just occurred here at work. Let them know our company security filed a report of the incident." I did exactly what he advised.

That was the first time I ever filed a report against someone harassing or attacking me. I was still in disbelief that it had even happened. I was outraged. My own father didn't raise his hand to me. How dare someone else do so!

The officer taking my complaint was kind and patient as he

asked me questions. "How long have you two been dating? Has he ever hit or threatened you before? What time did it happen? How long were you on the highway in the car? Was there anyone else in the house when he took you to the basement? Did you tell your parents what happened?"

I was surprised how compassionate he was. He seemed to sense that I was a "good girl from a decent family." And, that this was new scary ground for me.

I don't know if the police reached out to JT or not. I didn't file paperwork for a restraining order; I don't recall that being discussed as an option.

After all of this, I decided to make my parents aware of what had transpired. Dad was angry, but calm. He said, "If you ever see JT around you, or following you, come directly home. Pull into the driveway, hitting the car horn. Stay in the car with the doors locked until one of us comes out. Your mother or I will immediately call 911 when we hear the horn blaring."

This is exactly what happened. I saw JT as I was approaching the house, so I pulled in and hit the horn. Dad called the police and then came out and escorted me into the house. There must have been a cruiser close by because the police stopped JT two blocks from our house. He had a gun in the car. They arrested him. He spent 30 days in jail. I never saw or heard from him again. Many years later, I heard that he had been shot by a relative and died.

Perhaps the real reason I left that insurance company was the discomfort and embarrassment I felt over that incident with JT. Maybe the denial of my vacation request just provided my mind with the escape mechanism.

SHATTERED

FREE FALL

"The Lord is close to the brokenhearted and saves those
who are crushed in spirit." – Psalm 34:18 NIV

Sometimes You Just Can't See What's Up Ahead

"In the world you will have tribulation. But take heart;
I have overcome the world." – John 16:33b ESV

I had been home from college, working full time since the summer of 1975. My brother David's body was discovered in March 1975. He took his own life shortly before his 24th birthday.

In 1979, I was working at the Kent County Health Department as part of their first lead abatement team. We provided information and resources regarding the danger of lead poisoning, especially to young children, along with abatement protocols for homes.

(Sidebar, it is now 2024. Kent County is currently advertising free water filters and lead abatement tools for residents.

Just last fall I saw Grand Rapids City workers removing lead pipes from the road that my grandchildren live on. Forty-four years later, the city, county, and the state have yet to rectify the lead problem in older homes. Why is that? Is it possibly because most of those homes are inhabited by Brown, Black, and/or poor folks?)

Back in 1979, we ran clinics at various locations around the city, while also providing testing in our mobile unit. We went out door-to-door in the high-risk areas of the city, sharing information and offering free testing to those aged five and younger. I was one of a team of four individuals. I really enjoyed the work, the flexibility, being outside, and the community contact.

One day, we had just come back to the office. We were filing reports and setting up our supplies for the next day when I was advised that there was a phone call for me. It was Mr. Porter, my debutante dad-substitute, one of my parents' closest friends.

"Debbie, you need to come home immediately."

"Why?" I asked. He repeated that I needed to come straight home. He sounded very tense and demanding.

"I'm not coming home unless you tell me what's going on. It's unusual for you to be calling me at work, something must have happened. I need to know what's going on. I'm not going to walk in blindly on something. I need to prepare myself. So, I need you to tell me what's happening or I'm not coming home." I sighed, exasperated by his lack of detail. I could feel myself beginning to shake internally as fear began creeping. What could have possibly happened that warranted a call from Warner, rather than Aunt Edna?

I don't recall how he phrased it. Did he say that there had been an accident? He did say that Daddy was dead. Did he say how? Surely not, or I don't think I would have gone home. Maybe he did and I went anyway for the sake of my mother.

"Your father is dead!"

I remember driving home and my mind not really being able to grasp it. I was 24. The only girl. Daddy's girl. I was clearly still a mental and emotional mess four years after my brother's suicide. Even today I wonder, *"Why did you call me home to see that? How did you think I could hold and process it?"* Intellectually, I realize that they were in shock. It was too much for them, even as adults. In a strange way, I was the most solid person in the family to deal with another tragedy despite my major dysfunctions.

I know that the Porters and my mother were in the house. There were just a few weeks left in the year. My younger brother, Albert, was in school at the University of Michigan. It wasn't time yet for his winter break.

I don't recall if anyone else was there. I don't even remember if the police were still there. They must have been, or, at least someone from the coroner's office, as the coroner must examine the body, perhaps there or perhaps at the morgue, prior to it being shipped to the funeral home.

What I do know is that the Porters and my mother were downstairs in the living room. My father was upstairs lying nude in the bathtub. *My bathtub,* mind you.

He was dead.

There was a TV tray next to the tub with a glass of water, vials knocked over, and an assortment of pills. This was, no doubt, the supply of psychotropic medicine he had been given over the years that had been stashed away in the kitchen cupboard.

There was a bit of blood on the floor and in the bathwater. He seemingly had become impatient while waiting for the pills to take effect. He had cut his wrist. However, he had done so only slightly, causing it to bleed but not deep enough to sever a vein or artery. It was the heavy dose of pills that killed him.

Imagine looking at your father, not only dead, but nude, lying in a bathtub. You probably can't even envision such a thing. No one should ever have to.

Decades later, during a winter break at seminary, I asked my spiritual director if we could do a marathon session so that I could revisit my brother and father's suicides.

We did. One of the things that I found helpful was being able to reframe many things at that stage of my life with her input. Three decades of life experience, the difference in perspective between a then 19- and 24-year-old compared to someone in their mid-50's, coupled with the wisdom, discernment, and peace of being in close relationship with the Lord for 18 years can significantly alter interpretations of life events.

I remember questioning why the bathtub of all places. She stated something to the effect of it being his last cry to be fully seen. Given pieces of his history and his brokenness that I am not sharing, that made sense to me.

Regardless, someone came and carried the body away. I have no memory of this, but I know that it happened.

The tub was now empty and the presenting question became "Who is going to clean up my bathroom?" I asked Aunt Edna, the level-headed woman of steel. She said, "No!" quite emphatically. It was like, I may want to, but I can't, not even for you.

By then, my brother Steve had arrived. He wouldn't come into the bathroom, but after much pleading on my part, he did sit at the top of the staircase outside the bathroom talking to me while I cleaned up everything.

I wonder now if I had moved my bedroom into the back room off of the bathroom yet, or if I was still in my original room. For the life of me, I can't remember. Did I have to walk through the bathroom daily to go to my bedroom? I guess it's irrelevant since I still had to use the bathroom every day. It's strange what we remember and what we forget.

Growing up, bathing was one of my favorite things. I loved taking warm bubble baths! Often, I would have a book to read, something to drink, and even a snack with me. I could stay in the tub for over an hour. When the water cooled, I would let some out and replace it with hot water, repeatedly.

I tried taking baths after Daddy died, but I couldn't. Even once I moved into my own place, with my own tub, it was still impossible. I always saw him lying in the tub. I shower. The only tub I can safely get into is a hot tub.

It's been decades now. I have wondered, now and then, if

perhaps I could bathe again after all these years. In fact, I did do oatmeal and cornstarch soaks about eight years ago when I had shingles. The discomfort of the shingles was stronger than the possibility of any mental images that might arise. They were quick soaks though, in and out, no lingering enjoying the bath as in days past.

I was shocked by my father's death. I never would have imagined that he might take his own life.

I believe that in addition to any depression or despair an individual may be experiencing, it takes a tremendous amount of courage and resolve to take your own life. I honestly saw my father as a weakling. This is partly because of his embarrassing kiss-ass, "yes sir master," shuffle performance in court some years prior when I escorted my mother to Grand Haven for his appearance.

I thought about his negative commentary on the Harlem Globetrotters for being (in his eyes) minstrels for White America. He refused to watch, or let us watch, their games on his TV.

The shuffle worked. The judge let him come home on probation. I lost any remaining respect I had for him on that day. It took decades for me to reacquire it along with the understanding, grace and forgiveness God has shed abroad in my heart.

I know that he fought many demons his entire life from growing up neglected by his mother, abused at boarding school, and again later during a random placement. I can't imagine the images that must have haunted him of the dead soldiers' bodies he collected during WWII to be shipped back home for burial. Not to mention his manic-depressive condition which worsened and intensified yearly.

He would periodically sit in the attic where David killed himself, near the black crate, smoking a joint. He would be up there sometimes for hours. I, on the other hand, would open the attic door and grab what I needed so fast you couldn't blink. I dreaded needing to go into the attic for anything. Everything that I had stored up there was on the right edge, as close to the door as possible.

My brother David's death was probably the straw that broke the camel's back. Dad couldn't, or didn't desire, to claw himself back from that loss. Perhaps he had reached the point that he was tired living with and fighting his own demons. Or, possibly he wanted to set my mother free.

I had begun encouraging her to get a divorce a couple of years prior to his death. She deserved to live a life without the stress and chaos. She refused to leave him.

I knew that they had met before she was a teenager. I knew she loved him. I imagine she married him before knowing the full extent of his mental health challenges.

She shared once that her family wanted her to marry Paul, a guy from a "well-to-do" family, but she wasn't attracted to him. She liked his younger brother. She couldn't disrespect the older brother by choosing the younger one. You didn't do that back then. I guess we still shouldn't do it today, but it wouldn't be as surprising.

Mom said that they predicted that Dad wouldn't amount to much. They told her she would have a bunch of kids and need their help. Her pride kept her from asking them for anything, despite the challenges she did encounter.

Once she told me of how she had walked blocks to the neighborhood market and then carried all the groceries home. When I was young, I never thought about how she got around when Daddy was absent or non-functional.

I thought she hadn't started driving until her late 40s or early 50s. Once when we were chatting, I mentioned how odd it was that she started driving so late in life. She laughed. "I started driving right after high school," she shared.

"Your father complained once about my driving. I told him that he could drive me then." From that day, until decades later, he was her personal chauffeur. He drove her to and from work and anywhere else she needed or desired to go. She and I may have had the same stubborn streak.

I confess, there were times when I had wished that dad would just disappear, but I never considered him dying.

I remember one time I was up early and began cleaning downstairs. He came down and began verbally harassing me because he wanted me to go back upstairs. I picked up one of the thick, heavy wooden candlestick holders that Bruce had brought mom from Jamaica. I reminded dad that I was not as crazy as him, but I wasn't scared of him. I was just slightly off enough to pop him upside his head if he didn't stop bothering me. He went upstairs and I finished cleaning.

My eldest brother, Bruce, who lived in Ypsilanti, came home for dad's memorial service. He had now lost his 2 best friends. David and Albert Sr.—brother and father. Steve and his family lived in town and were present. Our youngest brother, Albert Jr., stayed at school. He did not attend dad's funeral.

Suppressed Emotional Detachment

"So, remove grief and anger from your heart and put away pain from your body, because childhood and the prime of life are fleeting." – Ecclesiastes 11:10 NASB

I don't know how to describe my state of being following my father's death. If my feet were crooked before, they were now snarled beyond recognition. I was hobbling along on stumps.

It's as if something started to slip off a shelf when David died, was caught, and pushed back on, although skewed. Now everything on the shelf came crashing down and the shelf along with it. Or, as if I tripped on a rug and caught myself following David's death and now, I not only tripped, but I tumbled down a flight of stairs.

It felt as if there wasn't anything beneath me. Nothing connecting me. No force to hold me in orbit. I was free floating, banging up against anything and everything, unanchored and significantly bruised.

RANDOM ACTS OF MADNESS

"Do not be deceived: "Bad company ruins good morals." – 1 Corinthians 15:33 ESV

Drifting

"For I know the plans I have for you," declares the Lord, "plans to prosper you and not to harm you, plans to give you hope and a future." – Jeremiah 29:11 NIV

It was springtime following Daddy's death. I'm not sure if I was working, or if so, where at. This may have been the time frame when I did my stint with VISTA volunteers. My conscious spiritual life was on pause. I was isolating. I was dangerously detached, mentally and emotionally.

I met Larry sometime during that winter. He was a slight distraction from the reality of my empty, painful life situation.

He was pleasant and funny. He had a vibrant, easy-going personality. He was good-looking and quite charismatic. I usually was attracted to men who were a bit darker, but every now and then I would go for someone who was light.

He had a history of viable employment, however, at that time he was operating primarily as a con-man, passing bad checks. I cashed a few for him at local stores. What did I care?

It was as if we were acting in someone else's plot; a storyline that made no sense. I am simply going through the motions of life at this time, yet even I knew how ridiculous some of his choices were. They were totally irrational, thus the image of a plot, perhaps something playing out in the *Twilight Zone*. If I could have discerned the madness in my present state, then something was truly off kilter.

Here's an example. Larry signed a lease for an apartment in a nice complex. He asked me if I would help furnish it. He was confused when I didn't. Ready for the kicker? He wrote a check for the deposit and first month's rent. It would only be a short matter of time before the check bounced. Even if he stalled with various excuses for a few weeks, he didn't have the funds to make the check good. He wouldn't be able to stay in the apartment. None of it made any sense to me. What was the purpose in getting the apartment?

It seemed like he was also choosing to live in a state of false reality. Perhaps his life was also more than he could face at that time. We were like two broken magnets being pulled towards one another.

The Highway Leading to Jail

"...for God is greater than our hearts, and he knows everything." – 1 John 3:20b CSB

Out of the blue, my mother asked me where I was going. I told her that I wasn't going anywhere. She waited a week, or so, and asked again. I gave the same reply. She said, "Please don't go off anywhere. It is not going to end well." I lied again, "Mom, I don't have any plans to travel." Yet I had already begun packing a few things to take on the trip.

Here's more insanity that should have been an indicator not to go on the trip even before my mother shared what she had "seen."

Larry bought a used Cadillac to drive down South and visit his brother at school. Yes, you guessed it. He wrote a check for the car. Oh, but it gets even crazier. He took the license plate off my Chevy Vega, the first car that I had ever purchased, and placed it on the Cadillac. Fine, I guess, unless a State Trooper happens to run the plate.

As the date approached which we were planning to leave, my mother approached me again, desperate to get through to me. She very calmly, yet emphatically stated that she has seen what is going to happen. She describes it as being like a scene in a movie.

"Debbie, you will be on the highway and the police cars will come from every direction. They are going to cross over the highway and surround you. They will throw open their doors, kneel behind them, and have long rifles pointing directly at the car."

Now mind you, except for seeing an expensive home with my husband on a ladder, my mother has never shared a vision with me that did not come to pass exactly as seen by her. She's batting 99.9% accuracy.

Larry and I drove down South. He checked in on his brother. We toured the campus and we headed back home.

Larry was driving. He noticed a trooper on the highway and slowed down. I admonished him for going too slow, stating that he was going to call attention to us. Finally, brilliant mind that I have, I told him to pull over and let me drive.

Almost immediately after making that switch, Mom's vision began to unfold. The trooper stopped us. He, no doubt, put the license plate number into the system which indicated a mismatch in vehicles.

They came from every direction. Behind us. From in front of us, crossing over the median. Pulling up beside us. Doors swung open and long shotguns were aimed at the car. It played out, to the letter, exactly as mother had shared.

We were placed in the officer's car. One of them drove the

Cadillac to the station. I was fingerprinted. I was placed in a large 2-person female cell with a divider across a portion of the space for privacy. It was across from the cell for minors.

There was a nice, young woman in the cell with me whose livelihood was from prostitution. We chatted a bit. She tried to calm my nerves.

"Try to relax. You're going to be ok. Have you ever been in trouble before? No. Well, this is what is going to happen. Since it's the weekend, you're stuck here. You will have to wait until Monday to go to court," she shared.

"Can I get a light?" I called out to the jail attendant. I was allowed to keep my cigarettes, but not my lighter. I needed a smoke, pronto!

I had not been officially charged with anything, even though I was the one driving the stolen vehicle.

They asked me if I wanted to make a phone call. I called Robin, my former college dorm mate, just so someone would know what had happened and where I was. I emphatically told her not to call anyone in my family. She disregarded this and called Bruce. She was then confused and angry when he said I had made my bed and would have to lie in it. I was furious with her. I knew he wouldn't help and didn't want my family, particularly my mother, to know.

Since they had confiscated my lighter, every 15 to 30 minutes I was asking them to light my cigarette. "Can I get a light?" "Can I get a light?" I was like a frenzied fiend.

On Saturday they asked me if I wanted to talk with a minister. I said no. Sunday morning, I called for the attendant. "I'm an Episcopalian. Do you think it would be possible to get a priest for me to talk to? If not, any minister will do."

I imagine that over time you get used to being locked up. You don't have a choice, really. But, that weekend, it was more than I could handle. I was already emotionally unglued and this was too much.

The minister came and met with me. "You seem like a nice young lady. I can't imagine how you got yourself in such a predicament. This guy must have really pulled the wool over your eyes. You should call home and let them know what's happening."

"Yes, thank you so much for stopping by to see me," I replied. "Please pray for me."

I will say this. God's grace was clearly present. We were stopped just outside the Cook County line and placed in this small town, "Mayberry" jail, rather than the massive Cook County jail system. God was not only with me, but also for me, even amid my follies.

Monday, we went to court. They kept Larry with plans of transferring him back to Michigan. He would be lodged in the Kent County Jail while the Grand Rapids police department pursued various charges against him.

"Miss, you're free to go."

"Excellent! I do have a few items in the car you confiscated," I shared, while asking how I was supposed to get home.

"Someone will take you to gather your things. We can drop you at either the bus or train station."

Not being ready to face my all-seeing mother just yet, I called an acquaintance from U of M who lived in Chicago. I needed to lay low a couple of days while I figured out where I could stay.

It had been 3 months since Dad died.

WALKING WITH A LIMP

LIFE GOES ON

*"And that, knowing the time, that now it is high time
to awake out of sleep: for now is our salvation nearer
than when we believed." – Romans 13:11 KJV*

Trying to Find My Way

*"Teach me thy way, O Lord, and lead me in a
plain path...." – Psalm 27:11 KJV*

I took the bus from Chicago back home to Grand Rapids. I
stayed at my Aunt Gwen's house for about two weeks.

I retrieved my Chevy Vega. I secured a new license plate, reporting that my previous one had been stolen. The car was parked
in her driveway with the hatch roof open. It snowed that night.
I was shocked, as it was the first week of April! This is the only
reason I remember the timing of these crazy events.

I went home. Mom and I picked up the pieces; she continued
to pray for me. I continued to stumble through life on auto-pilot,
trying not to cause any permanent damage.

As I look back over my late-teen years, I see the duality reflected
in my personality as I attempt to "discover" myself. I am many

things: cross-cultural, a want to be militant, the prissy debutante, somewhat of an urban hippie, the emerging scholar. I'm becoming aware that I can choose who people see.

One of the things that I enjoyed about being at the University of Michigan was that there were only a few people who knew me. I could wake up in the morning and decide how I wanted to present myself to the world. Middle-class, preppie, militant with a big afro, a hippie swagger, regular, or whatever. I had the freedom to explore different expressions of myself by altering my attire and my hair.

Regardless of my outer appearance, there was an aura or something that exuded from me. I was generally well received by the public at large. I always experienced excellent service when I was out and about. I met interesting folks. I enjoyed varied encounters and conversations. I was generally pleasant and charming.

This is who the priest at the jail saw and responded so kindly to. I carried myself as if I came from a 'good family.'

It is why when I got caught shoplifting at Briarwood Mall, in Ann Arbor, their security chief was so surprised and accommodating.

This occurred shortly after I rejoined the world following my brother's suicide. I'm not sure what compelled me to slip the pair of jeans into a package I was carrying. When they stopped me exiting the store and retrieved them, I was annoyed that I had been caught. I offered to pay for the jeans. They refused to accept my money, instead calling the mall security. He secured my personal information and I returned to the dorm.

Later the following week, the phone rang in the dorm. "Hello."

"Yes, hello. This is Mr. Jones calling. I'm in charge of security at Briarwood Mall. I was so shocked the store reported you for shoplifting. I see you frequently at the mall, shopping, or hanging out with friends grabbing a bite to eat. You seem like such a nice young lady. It's obvious that you come from a decent home. I couldn't believe it when I saw that you were the perpetrator. The store reported that you had sufficient funds to purchase the item, so I am really confused."

"I am so embarrassed and sorry! I've been a mess since my brother's unexpected death over spring break. He committed suicide."

"Sorry for your loss, especially the terrific manner of his death. I understand you're perhaps feeling lost right now. However, you must realize that acting out is not going to help."

"Yes, I know." He gave me a friendly scolding and cautioned me that it couldn't happen again. "No, it won't. Thank you so much for giving me a warning."

This proper young lady from a decent family is who the Grand Rapids Police lieutenant saw upon my return from Chicago, too. He knew that I had passed some of the small fraudulent checks for Larry. He didn't really care. He wrote it off as a nice girl being manipulated and taken advantage of by a shyster.

He had been tracking Larry for a while, securing the necessary proofs for charges. He was baffled by the trip down South. "What was the purpose behind it? Did he commit crimes down there too?"

I laughed. "No," I replied. "He simply went to visit his younger brother at school. He was proud of him. He wanted to see how he was doing, to know that everything was alright." The officer thanked me and that was the end of my role in the highway drama.

A Semi-Permanent Limp

"Whoever walks in integrity walks securely, but whoever takes crooked paths will be found out." – Proverbs 10:9 NIV

I don't know about other fractured, wounded people, but I wasn't stable. At least my personal, emotional self wasn't. I could perform well on a job. I continued to excel in school years later when I returned.

My relational self was on a rollercoaster or tilt-a-whirl. Perhaps not daily, but certainly too often.

When it all became too much, I self-medicated with marijuana and/or sex, hoping the sex would be satisfying. Too often it wasn't.

Years later, there was a short period when I drank too much, and a 6-month period that I added cocaine to the mix which was a volatile combination.

AS THE WORLD TURNS

"And the world is passing away along with its desires, but whoever does the will of God abides forever." – 1 John 2:17 ESV

An Encounter with an Unexpected Outcome

"I can do all things through him who strengthens me." – Philippians 4:13 ESV

I don't track time well. It is one effect of the post-traumatic stress I have experienced. I have difficulty sequencing events. This exercise in writing my story is causing me to slowly unravel events and place them in their proper time frame. Often, I must use a specific event that occurred, like giving birth, to place myself within a given year or decade. I can then sometimes look backwards from that point to recall what else happened that particular year.

The summer of 1981 brought new opportunities and new connections. It was the year following so many hard changes - my father's death and my brief jail excursion. My cousin Janice, who was living in Detroit at the time, invited my mother and I to attend a soiree she was hosting for Granada's Ambassador. My mother thoroughly enjoyed this type of outing. It was a great, positive mother-daughter weekend for us to bond and embrace the thread of normalcy that still existed in our relationship.

Janice's home was perfect to host such an event with its massive living room, dining room, sitting room, and screened porch area. Her antique décor was mixed with a few colorful contemporary pieces and a large collection of paintings and artifacts from Black and/or African artists. We met late afternoon with people coming and going through the evening. Everyone was dressed in chic summer outfits and looked amazing! The catering was handled by one of Janice's personal friends who served a mix of mouth-watering Caribbean and Southern dishes and exotic drink selections.

One of my cousin's dear friends was an older photographer who was capturing the event on film for her. Dan was enamored with me. He foolishly lavished flattery towards me as he tried to lure me with the bait of creating a portfolio for me. He hoped that I might be enticed with the prospect of him introducing me in circles that might offer an opportunity for a modeling gig.

Given my typical bored and aimless state of mind, I took him up on his offer. I returned one weekend with a variety of outfits appropriate for photo shoots in various locations around the city. It was a carefree time of make believe for me, amusing and fun.

I remember him introducing me to various individuals that he thought would impress me. He took a photo of me with Don King, the boxing promoter. Dan was surprised and confused when he became aware that I was looking away from Don as he snapped the picture. I love boxing, especially Muhammad Ali, but I couldn't have cared less about Mr. King.

Dan was trying to excite me with the possibility of being a "Ring Girl" for the next fight. This involved strutting around the ring, smiling and holding a card announcing the next round. He had no idea that there was no way in hell I would ever parade my flat-chested, skinny leg frame, scantily garbed in front of a large crowd.

Although I enjoyed pretty things and nice places, I was not impressed with folks based upon their income or positions.

A Life Altering Relationship

"Let marriage be held in honor among all, and let the marriage bed be undefiled, for God will judge the sexually immoral and adulterous." – Hebrews 13:4 ESV

One of the individuals Dan tried to impress me with was a human resource director at a fairly large industrial paint plant.

He was attractive, intelligent, confident, and seemed easy going with a sense of humor. After introductions and some shared conversation, I excused Dan from the room so that I could speak with Charles one-on-one. We arranged to meet later for a drink.

It was as simple as that. We met. There was a mutual attraction. We shared phone numbers. Neither asked if the other was married or involved in a serious relationship. We enjoyed one another's presence and conversation. We began calling one another. I would pop up in Detroit. He would take me out for dinner and a cocktail.

Later that summer I joined him driving out to Denver. If memory serves me correctly, he was attending a N.A.A.C.P. convention. I explored the city while he attended sessions. We hung out late afternoons and evenings.

I was instructed not to answer the hotel phone. This meant he was either married or involved with someone. The phone rang, so of course I answered it. She introduced herself using his surname. It turns out that they just so happened to have the same last name. She wasn't his wife. I later found out that he did have a wife. A wife, a girlfriend, and working on having me. Oh, my!

He was 9 ½ years older than me. I enjoyed his company. I didn't have any qualms about being with a married man. I was a total wreck and not looking for a serious relationship. Married men were convenient since they couldn't be around too much or get seriously hung up on you. Or, so I thought. I was merely floating along from one thing to the next.

At some point he came to Grand Rapids, met my mother, packed me up and moved me to Detroit. He gave me a boring job coding paints which didn't last long. The woman with his same surname worked there too. What a charade!

How had I gone from, "How dare you stop by to see me on your way to someone else's house?" with Thomas, to simply not caring what was going on in any man's life? I daresay it was losing all sense of stability in my world and not being in touch with myself following my brother and father's suicides. Nothing truly mattered. I was merely going through the motions of living.

I was aware enough of my body, however, such that I knew the moment I conceived. The doctor gave me a due date that was off a few weeks. I knew exactly the evening I became pregnant.

God told me to keep the baby.

Yes, He talks to us even when we are living wrong. If he didn't, no one would ever hear His voice. We all fall short, even those who think they are perfect and without sin.

Charles asked me to have an abortion. Eventually I relented to his constant pestering. I scheduled an appointment back home in Grand Rapids.

The nurse, and then the doctor, were surprised and murmuring with one another. "Is there something wrong? Is the baby all right?" I inquired.

"Tell me again how far along the doctor in Detroit said you were?" I reiterated the date the physician in Detroit had given me.

"I'm not certain that's correct," he responded. "You appear to be further along than that. I'm going to do an ultrasound so we can accurately determine how many weeks you are."

"I told the other doctor when I conceived. I knew the moment it happened. He told me that was impossible." I shared my actual conception date with this doctor. The ultrasound confirmed that date.

The nurse advised that they couldn't do the procedure, however, I could return to Detroit and have a procedure done in a hospital there.

"Oh, no! I will not have them induce my child and then kill him! I shouldn't even be here. It will work itself out."

The nurse was surprised by my response! "Do you need a list of resources to assist with the pregnancy or baby items?"

"No, no. We'll be just fine. Thank you."

I knew I wasn't supposed to be having an abortion. God had told me to have this child, so He would make a way. Relieved, I dressed and made my way back to Detroit to alert Charles of the change in developments.

MAJOR CHANGE

"Jesus said, "Let the little children come to me, and do not hinder them, for the kingdom of heaven belongs to such as these." – Matthew 19:14 NIV

Motherhood

"Behold, children are a heritage from the Lord, the fruit of the womb a reward." – Psalm 127:3 ESV

I could see and feel the physical changes beginning; however, my stomach was still small enough that others couldn't tell that I was pregnant.

I came back to my mother's house for Thanksgiving. I shared with her that I was pregnant and asked if I could move back in with her. I needed to secure employment before my pregnancy became apparent. She agreed.

Charles was in touch sporadically during my pregnancy, visiting me occasionally.

We had a terrible snow storm the weekend I went into labor. Mother was out East for a funeral. The highways, if not closed, were mostly impassable from all reports.

Shortly after midnight, so that Monday morning, my water broke. I took a shower and packed a bag. I called mom. She told me to, "Call Edna and ask her if she will accompany you to the hospital."

I phoned and woke her up. I shared that I was having contractions and thought it was time to go to the hospital. I asked her if she might be willing to accompany me since mom was still out of town. She responded, "Yes, of course. Just give me 15 or 20 minutes to get myself together." (Aunt Edna did not drive.)

We had heavy, wooden garage doors that had to be manually opened. There was at least a foot of snow in the driveway with the snow drifts.

By the grace of God, I opened and closed the garage doors. I drove the four blocks to pick her up and proceeded to drive myself to Butterworth Hospital. An attendant parked the car for me while another seated me in a wheelchair and took me inside.

By now it was perhaps around 4:00 am. Around 9:00 or 10:00 am, I encouraged Aunt Edna to go home. She was tired and needed her rest. I convinced her that I would be fine. I would let her know once I delivered.

I had left a message for Charles, but I knew that it was probably impossible for him to make it over from Detroit to Grand Rapids in the blizzard.

David Charles waited until his dad arrived. When he walked in the room, the nurse asked Charles if he had completed the parenting classes that were required for him to be present for the birth. The doctor looked at this imposing man in his late 30s and told the nurse to get him a gown and cap.

Upon hearing his father's voice in the room, my son's head began to crown. Charles was telling me to open my eyes and watch in the mirror above me. Truly amazing!

Charles hung around for the day. He, I believe intentionally, neglected to sign the required paperwork so that he would be listed as David's father.

I ended up having to force his hand on this issue by filing a paternity suit. His name was placed on my son's birth certificate. The downside for Charles was that by forcing me to go this route it threw him automatically into the system requiring that child support payments be established. Eventually we came to an agreement, I wrote off thousands of dollars in arrears, and we handled things outside of the system.

They cleaned up my beautiful, baby boy, counted his toes and fingers, completed his Apgar scale and whatever other screenings were required, and laid him on my chest. He immediately began breast-feeding.

There aren't words to describe that moment. I will simply say that the empty shell that I had become was flooded with emotions. I woke up. Intellectually I didn't know if I was up to this momentous task; I didn't know if I was too damaged. However, I was filled with joy for the first time in several years.

I was 27 that year, on March 21st, the day David Charles was born. I will turn 28 that September. My father took his life in December 1979, 4 years and 9 months after my brother David had taken his, and was discovered that first week of March in 1975.

I had been wandering blind, crippled, lost in the wilderness of despair for 8 long years. I wasn't yet aware, but it was no way near being over.

My mother returned from New Jersey. She entered my hospital room and said, "Your father would be so disappointed." She didn't ask how I felt. She didn't tell me that my son was beautiful. No. She let me know that my father would be disappointed because I had a child out of wedlock.

I wanted to reply that I was disappointed that my dad was a pervert. I was disappointed that he killed himself lying naked in the bathtub. I was disappointed that they allowed me to see him like that.

Instead, I said, "Have you seen the baby? Isn't he gorgeous?!"

She didn't reply. She was upset that I was naming him David after my brother. "You can't bring him back. My David is gone."

"I know that. I realize he can't be replaced. I want to honor him. I am going to name my child David even though you don't want me to. He will have a different middle name and his father's last name. There will only be one David Alan McCreary. I am not going to change my mind or bend on this."

My beautiful baby boy, David and I went home to live with her. We, or rather I, was going to have to muddle through it all. Mom was both disappointed and embarrassed that I had a child out-of-wedlock. It was initially quite a struggle for her to hold those feelings while trying to accept the reality. She tried to be supportive in her own ways. She doted on David and was protective towards him. He adored her growing up. He still does, even though she is no longer with us. When he was older, he loved going up North to the cottage with her and her friend, Homer. Homer would take him out on the pontoon and teach him how to fish.

Overall, mom was a good "Granny" and a great help to me, especially those first few years. She didn't approve of me though. I was a negative stigma on the family, more so I think in her mind, than my brother and father who had taken their own lives. They were gone so perhaps it was easier to forgive them.

The first years went relatively well. I worked, came home, and parented my son. I loved taking him to the park, over to Grand Haven for boat rides, hanging out at the beach, sharing the outdoors things I enjoyed with him, and participating in various children's activities and events throughout the city. I gave him what I had received growing up.

Parenting

"Remember not the sins of my youth or my transgressions;
according to your steadfast love remember me, for the
sake of your goodness, O Lord!" – Psalm 25:7 ESV

Things changed once I started taking classes two evenings per week. My mother would keep David if I had a work function and/or to allow me to attend school. It was more of a rarity for her to do so for me to engage socially.

David loved being with her, but he resented the disruption to our normal routine. He didn't like me leaving to go to school. He liked it even less if I hung out late after school. He began to act out. He was disruptive, knocking things over or destroying things to vent his displeasure.

I had no idea how to proceed. I began to emotionally detach. At one point, when he was around 8 or 9 years old, he and I were doing family therapy. During one of our sessions the counselor said that although my mother loved us both, the underlying tensions she had with me, coupled with our dual messages to my son, made it impossible for he and I to work anything out.

He shared that if I wanted things to be different and better, I needed to get my own place. I started looking. I eventually found a brand-new duplex on Philadelphia Avenue near the elementary school David was attending.

The first time my brother Bruce saw David Charles, as an infant, he asked if he could have him. This was out of the question. However, at one point when he was still a baby, I packed us up and moved down to Ypsilanti to stay with him, and Val, his wife at that time.

I was trying not only to be apart from my mother's influence, but also to be closer to Charles, although I certainly wouldn't have admitted that last bit at the time.

I secured a job at the Methodist Children's Home Society, a residential treatment facility for children, in Detroit. I worked the 2nd or 3rd shifts. I secured a wonderful woman to keep David while I was working.

This arrangement was a mixed bag. I don't recall how long it lasted – perhaps around six months. It was difficult switching from the 2nd shift to the midnight shift at work. I would pick up David around 8:30 am. and of course I was ready to go to sleep.

Sometimes my brother, Bruce, would watch the baby while I got a few hours of sleep. Other times I had to nap when David did. This lasted for a couple of months until I was surprisingly relieved from working the overnight shift. I stood up one morning and my foot went out on me. It must have been asleep. It was such a freak accident. Somehow, I must have twisted it or stepped down wrong on it. As I moved about completing my shift, the foot became swollen and painful. I filed an injury report at work.

I made it home to Bruce's and asked him to watch David Charles while I went to get an x-ray. It was such a bizarre injury. I had fractured 2 or 3 small bones in the top of my left foot. They put a walking cast on up to my knee. I was unable to work for 6 to 8 weeks. I collected unemployment.

David and I spent much of my recovery time back in Grand Rapids. I decided that was where I needed to be for stability even if peace of mind proved to be allusive.

Some of those early years are fuzzy. At one point, I did the stint with the VISTA volunteer program working on a community project with neighborhood centers. Our training took place in Lansing. One of the guys I met over there worked the sound stage for big concerts as a side gig.

He invited me up north to Castle Farms in Charlevoix, Michigan. Concerts and other events were held in 'The Castle.' The Temptations were performing. I could bring along a friend and attend free of charge. I had a raggedy piece of car at the time. Anyone in their right mind would not have driven it that far. I, of course, didn't think twice about it. I called Rae, Daun's younger sister, and the two of us headed up North for the free concert.

While waiting around for my friend to finish up with the stage crew, so that we could thank him again before taking off, members of the Temptations began coming out to their bus. A couple of them started talking to us.

We stayed up North much longer than we should have. We ran out of gas on the way home. Thankfully someone assisted us. I had left my sleeping son at home. I returned barely in time for my mother to make it to work. She was livid!

This is just one example of how careless and inconsiderate I could be floating along in the moment, not being rational. I suppose in my way of thinking I knew David was fine at home with Granny. I certainly thought I would be home well before he awakened in the morning. I believed I needed a break. No foul, no harm.

One of the Temptations had invited us over to Detroit the following week. I remember hanging out in their suite and the fire alarm going off in the hotel. Many months later, Ollie called to let me know they were doing a show in Grand Rapids. He wondered if I would like to come out for dinner and the show.

I didn't see him again until many years later. I was in Toronto with a friend for the Caribana Carnival. We were walking across a bridgeway in a facility. Ollie was approaching us with a woman on each arm. Our eyes locked for a moment, but we didn't speak.

My friend said, "He knows you." I inquired why he thought so. "I saw him look at you and the quick gaze of recognition when we passed one another."

I said, "Yes, we hung out a couple of times." He said something to the effect of that was the type of person I should be with, a celebrity, someone with money and access to places and things.

I was like, "Nah, I have no interest in hanging on a guy's arm that has another woman on the other arm." I'm thinking, it's rough enough knowing that most guys are not monogamous. I certainly don't desire to openly share a guy with another woman.

AN ILLUSION OF NORMALCY

STABILITY? NOT JUST YET

*"O that my ways may be established to keep
your statutes!"* – Psalm 119:5 NASB

A Significant Shift

*"Forget the former things; do not dwell on the past. See,
I am doing a new thing! Now it springs up; do you not
perceive it? I am making a way in the wilderness and
streams in the wasteland."* – Isaiah 43:18-19 NIV

The concert up North, the Temptations, and Toronto are all random. I guess I'm sharing it because it helped me figure out some timelines.

We have arrived at the point where I was working at Blue Care Network. I didn't like it there. I had just applied for and been offered a job at a different company.

When I told one of my close co-workers, she called her husband over at Blue Cross Blue Shield of Michigan. He was a manager in their marketing department. She asked him to bring me over there, which he did even though he didn't really have an open position for me.

I eventually transferred into customer service. I remained at BCBSM for almost 10 years. I tried to lean into the form of stability motherhood both provided and required.

Friendship

"Perfume and incense bring joy to the heart, and the pleasantness of a friend spring from their heartfelt advice." – Proverbs 27:9 NIV

One of the gifts and blessings from BCBSM was meeting my best friend Marian, aka Mikki. She and I attended training together in Detroit. Since we were both Black and didn't know anyone else, we signed up to room together. We immediately clicked, as if we had grown up knowing one another.

Our friendship was one of the greatest gifts from God in my lifetime. It was as if I had been tossed a lifejacket or buoy to remain afloat until my day of reckoning and being overtaken by the Spirit of God.

Mikki was a real friend. She loved and accepted me unconditionally, warts and all. She called me out, challenging me, correcting me, and telling me when I was just flat out wrong. She gently and lovingly embraced and comforted me at times when the world was too much for me.

She trusted me with her story, her true self, believing that I would accept her unconditionally as well. Which I did.

We shared most of our stories, secrets, dreams, and desires with one another. We celebrated victories together, commiserate over our hurts and disappointment, partaking of one another's joys and laments.

Her husband was a bit of a recluse and not socially active apart from family get-togethers, so she and I attended all sorts of things together ranging from movies, concerts, plays, community events, to just having a cocktail at one of the local spots.

We talked daily, at work, and after work too. She was the sister that I never had, intricately connected to every facet of my life, and I hers.

I became interwoven in her family attending various holidays, picnics, and events. I was Aunt Debbie to her children and she was Aunt Mikki to my son.

She was also a lifeline when my imbalanced, dysfunctional side reached its maximum capacity juggling the responsibility of parenting and normal life. She would take 'her boy' David to give me a break, but also, in truth, to protect us both from one another in the moment. Not that I would physically harm him, but to buffer the emotional damage, especially if either one of us was acting out having a tantrum.

Most of all, she let me know that even with my brokenness, I have value. I believe it is why, many years later, I was drawn to a particular postcard. It has a picture of a beautiful green porcelain bowl. The bowl has a significant crack that has been repaired with gold.

The message reads, "In Japan, broken objects are often repaired with gold. The flaw is seen as a unique piece of the object's history, which adds to its beauty. Consider this when you feel broken."

Mikki allowed me to frequently consider that about myself over our 3-decade friendship prior to her passing. The memory of her continues to feed my soul even today.

The Blues

"Whatever you do, work at it with all your heart, as working for the Lord, not for human masters." – Colossians 3:23 NIV

I liked working in customer service. There was a sense of satisfaction helping people get the most out of their health insurance benefits and guiding them through the bureaucratic red-tape, obstacles, and minutiae inherent in the industry.

Many people are intimidated by large, corporate industries. They may not understand their policies and benefits. They may be afraid to ask questions, or to even know what questions to ask. For example, a surgery bill may be rejected, even though the procedure is a covered benefit. The individual struggles to pay for the procedure even though they can't afford it. The claim was only rejected because the surgeon's office failed to submit a copy of the surgical report along with the charge. The average person doesn't know this.

I was good at my job. I am constituted such that most things that I am good at or that come easily to me, I can complete much faster than others while maintaining quality. Or, at least I could when I was younger.

This was a problem. A union representative approached me and said I was answering too many customer calls each day. I was perplexed. I was informed that my high call volume was skewing the office statistics. If I didn't slow down, they were going to raise the quota for the customer service reps which would be problematic. I was told to stop 'showing off' as it wouldn't bode well for me.

I replied that I understood. However, I wasn't trying to prove anything to anyone. I was working at my normal speed. I couldn't really control or modify that flow. Yet, I was clear as to the problem it was creating. I had a viable solution. I could meet and/or exceed our daily quota by lunchtime, or shortly thereafter.

My solution—after lunch, or early afternoon, I would come off the phone. Our written caseload, writing up the customer issues and submitting them for reprocessing/correction, was always backlogged; I would work on those. This solved the union's issue and our supervisor loved it.

I began to function as the assistant supervisor in our office without having the title or the upgraded pay. It was fine. Jane appreciated me and began trying to determine how she could upgrade me within the union system since I didn't have the greatest seniority. When that time came the rep with the most seniority allowed me to bid and have the position.

I was open and honest with Jane. Much more so than she preferred. Our office at this time was situated out by Ramblewood Apartments. There were paths through the trees that you could walk through.

Often during the nice weather months, I would take a walk during a break or lunch hour so that I could hit a joint a few times. I did not share this with Jane. I did let her know when I was going over to the restaurant to take a break and have a drink. She would always say, "I don't want to know. Don't tell me these things." I would laugh and respond, "I just want you to know that I will be out of the office for a bit." To which she would reply, "Then just tell me that. I don't need to know what you're doing."

Jane was a great person and supervisor. She cared about her people as well as the job. She always celebrated special occasions in the office. She gave us nice, thoughtful gifts for Christmas. She knew that I had her back. I wanted our office to do well.

I do remember one perplexing moment though. One summer she invited a few of us out to her boat which was docked in Holland. I love the water, so I was really looking forward to this. We arrived and were hanging out on the boat. Folks had brought snacks and drinks. Finally, I inquired when we were going to take the boat out. Jane replied something to the effect that we weren't. She just liked to sit out here on the boat. I thought, *"WTF! No one came over here just to sit on a boat and not go out on the water!"*

I liked Jane though. I was glad that I wasn't reporting to her when after 10 years I quit without giving notice.

I was the first person of color to become a supervisor in West Michigan. The home office in Detroit had numerous people of color in various positions. West Michigan had been proud of keeping us out. That began to shift once we began reporting to a regional director from the Lansing office who was Black.

At one point management was identifying folks who weren't meeting quota standards. They identified my best friend, Marian, in this group. Her pace was slower than some others, but she was an excellent customer service representative.

Her patience with the customer was good. She was personable while maintaining professionalism. She was very thorough investigating and resolving her casework. Her quality was excellent.

I made the mistake of warning her that she was being watched. Rather than her receiving that as coming from friend to friend— she took it as supervisor to employee. She reported it to the union for protection. This caused the first riff ever in our friendship. We had been 'besties' for about 7 or 8 years. This was a major break. We muddled through it and got back on proper footing.

I was a supervisor in a union shop. Upper management would outline strategies and initiatives for change that they would have the supervisors introduce to the staff. This protected them, giving them leeway to change their position without the union or employees realizing it.

I don't recall what change was being suggested, but the union pushed back. It became a heated contention. The supervisors were thrown to the lions. The management team halted their proceedings saving face.

Rather than taking 'a hit' for the management team, I bucked the system. I called them out to the union and employees, exposing their plans and deceptiveness. I became a 'marked' person within the management ranks. It would only be a matter of time before they made their move against me.

All Is Not as It Appears

*"He shapes the hearts of each; He considers all
their works." – Psalm 33:15 BSB*

My life took on some semblance of normalcy with an established flow during these years. Again, parenting grounded me
to a large degree.

At one point, as I previously mentioned, I began taking night
classes at Aquinas College. They had a very flexible evening and
weekend schedule for older, working adults. I discovered that my
Pell Grant didn't have an expiration date for private colleges. I
was able to use it along with the tuition reimbursement benefit
that BCBSM offered.

I attended on and off, beginning while I was at Blue Cross, and
finishing many years later when I was working at the Gerald R.
Ford Job Corps Center. At that point I needed about 15 credits,
only 5 classes, to complete my degree, so it didn't make sense
not to return to school.

I continued pursuing a psychology major. I also ended up with
enough courses to have a dual major in sociology. My electives
were surprisingly filled with religious study courses. I remember
trying to sign up for the next religion class and my advisor telling
me that I had used up all my available elective credits. She inquired
if I wanted to switch my major or minor. I said no. Many years
later the impetus behind taking the courses would be revealed.

I began my university/college trek in September, 1973. I obtained my Bachelor of Arts degree with honors in the spring of
2002. It's never too late. God does, and will, redeem the time.
If we allow Him.

CRUSHED

THE INSTABILITY OF BROKENESS

*"Why do you go around so much changing
your way?" – Jeremiah 2:36a NASB*

Aimless Wandering

*"She does not keep straight to the path of life; her ways
wander, and she does not know it." – Proverbs 5:6 NRSV*

I knew I was unstable. I knew I wandered. I didn't know how
to prevent it. Even if there were long periods of seeming stability,
the crushing weight of guilt, shame, remorse, hopelessness, despair,
anguish, darkness, loneliness, disbelief, uncertainty, direction-
lessness, negative thoughts, a racing mind, and restless, sleepless
nights would eventually lure me into self-medicating. It was the
only way I knew to quiet my mind and emotions for a moment.

It was a Catch-22. The very things that would cause a momentary calm were the same things that created and fed the dark
sphere that had me ensnared. It was a relentless, vicious cycle.

I had brief, very random encounters with my son's father until
I graduated from seminary. Initially these were very unhealthy
and compounded my feelings of low self-esteem. I did enjoy the

long-weekend in Boston once he moved out East, reportedly
for a new employment position. I liked to travel and had never
been in that area before. We did a bit of sight-seeing, went out
to dinner, and attended a concert with Dionne Warwick.

I walked away from these encounters feeling guilt, wearing a
heavy cloak of unworthiness. I eventually stopped engaging in
sexual relations with him. We were able to shift and maintain
contact regarding our son.

I dated a news reporter when David was young, under the
age of five. We kept bumping into one another at community
functions. He eventually introduced himself and asked me out.

We had a semi-normal friendship. We enjoyed one another's
company and hanging out together. We had similar interests. He
could get quite angry, not towards me, but with other things,
like work. I remember one time his hand was bruised. When I
inquired what had happened, he shared something that happened
at work. His response was to hit his hand on the steering wheel,
repeatedly, out of frustration. He also had a latent fear that at any
time he might become schizophrenic like his brother. Eventually
we fizzled out and stopped seeing one another. I didn't trust men,
nor did I value myself. This was a dangerous, toxic combination.
I hung out with a couple of guys randomly over the years. These
were unhealthy individuals for me, who also drank and/or used
marijuana. Marijuana was my drug of choice at that time. I was
primarily a social drinker. That is, until my heart was broken.

I met a great guy during one of my periods of normalcy when
I was attending school. Mikki took me over to his table in the
club and introduced us. He was divorced and up front about
not desiring to get into a serious relationship. That was fine. I
knew I was a mess and had no interest in trying to be in a "real"
relationship with anyone.

He had seen me around town. He was familiar with a few
of the positive aspects of my life, such as my social and church
activities. As such, he was attracted to my presenting persona.

He wasn't aware of the dysfunctional mess I was just below the surface. This is the guy I was with in Toronto. The kicker was that he was the type of person I would have wanted to be with if I was 'normal." I unwittingly fell in love.

I learned that he was seeing another woman in a nearby city. He had been seeing her first, apparently for some time.

Bill began giving me signs that he was going to stop seeing me. We were scheduled to travel to Jamaica, but he wanted to cancel the trip. I advised that everything was already paid for and suggested that we go have a good time before deciding if we were going to call it quits.

We had a great time. We did all the typical sight-seeing venues in Montego Bay where we stayed, including a day trip to walk the rocks in Ocho Rios. We took the local bus to Negril, as I was insistent on seeing Rick's Cafe.

My brother Bruce went to Jamaica many times over the years for decades. I had heard so many stories about Negril. He shared meeting Michael Manley, before he became Prime Minister, and the conversations they shared at Rick's. I couldn't be that close and not go there.

I found out that the local bus stopped right outside our hotel. I decided I would take the bus down to Negril. Bill didn't want to go. I went ahead and checked out the schedule and made plans to go that Thursday.

I woke up early that morning, excited about the adventure to Negril! Bill said, "So what are we doing today?" I responded, "I told you. I'm taking the bus down to Negril." He shared that he didn't feel comfortable or safe doing that. I said, "Well you should stay back and hang out here at the hotel then. I'm going to see Rick's Café." He felt like he had to be the "protective" male, so he relented and came along with me.

Negril was great. It turned out to be my friend's favorite day out of our week on the island. He thoroughly enjoyed the conversations on the bus with the local folks. The beach in Negril is as beautiful as I had heard. I could sense my brother's presence sitting in Rick's Café ordering a cocktail.

The trip didn't change Bill's mind about the direction he was leaning towards with us though. When we returned, he let me know that we should take a break and not see one another.

I stopped by one weekend without announcing myself. I was high and wanted to see him. His other female friend was there. I became jealous and enraged even though he had made it clear he didn't desire to be in a committed relationship. I slashed one of his tires and left. That, of course, was pretty much the end of our times together.

There were random times when I would show up drunk, late at night after leaving the bar. I would ring the bell or knock hard a few times; and every now and then he would let me in for the night. Eventually it came to a complete stop. If I was depressed with low self-esteem prior to this relationship, I have now plummeted to new depths.

My mother and Mikki helped with my son because I wasn't reliable. I worked and provided meals. I did the routine things. But I wasn't emotionally stable or available in the ways that I should have been. I became detached. I didn't have the capacity or wherewithal to hold this new pain and disappointment. I spiraled out of control. I stopped taking classes. I had stopped smoking marijuana upon returning from Jamaica. I started to drink more. I began to isolate and shut myself in at home. I was totally depressed. I felt like a total loser and wondered what the point of it all was.

GOD, IT'S ME, DEBBIE. ARE YOU THERE?

"Where can I go from your Spirit? Where can I flee from your Presence?" – Psalm 139:7a NIV

Where Was God?

"Their heart is faithless; now they must bear their guilt. The Lord will break down their altars, and destroy their sacred pillars." – Deuteronomy 12:3 NASB

The psalmist says that if he ascends to heaven, God is there. If he makes his bed in Sheol (abode of the dead), God is there, too.

I love the line from the movie, *The Count of Monte Cristo,* "God is in everything…even in a kiss."

God is in everything. He was present in my dysfunctional mess.

One of my coworkers had been friends with Mikki when the two of them first had their children. She was married, but liked to hang out. She had graduated from drinking and using marijuana to using cocaine, as well.

One of the men she knew was curious about me. She arranged

our meeting one evening when we left the club. My son was spending the night with a friend. We came back to my place to kick it. He pulled out some cocaine. They persuaded me to try it.

Initially, I was very apprehensive and only used a small amount. Over time, as I began spending time with them, I began using more.

She knew his wife from back in the day. She decided it was more advantageous to be friends with them, as a couple, than to hang out with me. They had more money, influence, and access to more social events.

Mikki also knew his wife. She asked me to stop seeing the guy. I refused. He had always cheated on his wife. The wife knew it. They knew it. So, what did it matter that he was cheating with me? It was the second time our friendship fractured. I believed it would be permanent this time.

He and I were consuming quite a bit of alcohol and cocaine. Our relationship became volatile. He was jealous, demanding, and becoming physically abusive. I was so high most of the time when not at work that I tolerated it. My self-esteem was non-existent at this point.

I tried to maintain a level of sobriety around my son and to shield him from my dysfunction. I didn't have a dissociative disorder, but I functioned as if I did. There were certainly two sides of me. I was the consummate professional and also a personal mess.

Do you remember Pig Pen in the Charlie Brown cartoons? He was always surrounded by a cloud of dirt. I, too, moved in a cloud. I was surrounded by a whirlwind of negative emotions. More than being surrounded, it felt like there was a heavy hand, or force, constantly pushing down on me whenever I was still. I could feel the weight of the shame, guilt, remorse, hopelessness, and despair. It imprisoned me. I didn't know how to free myself.

I purposed to break free from the toxic relationship I was in. The more nonchalant and unavailable I became, the more possessive and violent he became. He would see me out having a good time and become furious.

It finally all came to a head late one Friday evening/early Saturday morning. He came by my place after I had left the club. This should have been a déjà vu moment for me from years prior. I guess I was too high or had now become too dysfunctional to think about it.

He was very soft spoken. This is more frightening than being yelled at. He quietly, politely began informing me of his rules and the new protocol he was establishing.

"You belong to me now. I am not going to let you go. I don't want you hanging around any other guys, even if they're just friends. I don't care that you're not sexually involved with them. You can't be around them. You're mine. I want you to stay home. When you finish work just come home. You may not go out to the clubs anymore. I better not see you in a club, even with your girlfriends."

My response did not bode well for me. I said, "I'm no longer interested in being with you or around you. You need to stay home with your wife, or hang out with whatever other woman catches your fancy. I'm done. It's time that I get myself together. I'm embarrassing to myself. Of course, I am going to hangout occasionally with my girlfriends. I'm not interested in seeing any other guys, but I can't do this with you anymore. I'm losing myself, more and more, each day."

He was livid! He picked up his beer bottle and began whacking me. I fought him off as much as I could. He eventually pronounced his edict one final time and left.

That Sunday, I was back down at the club. There was a light crowd out that evening. The back room was closed. I stepped back there with someone to toot some cocaine. When I came out into the main room he was there.

He immediately approached me. "I just gave you clear instructions. What did I tell you? You need to go home immediately."

I was high. I responded with a clever retort and tapped the bottom of his drink. Apparently too hard. It inadvertently hit his tooth. He hit me with his fist on the side of my head. I fell to the ground. I got up searching the tables for a beer bottle to crack him upside his head.

People came rushing towards us, breaking us apart. They circled him to prevent him from getting to me. I was escorted out to my car and asked if I was OK to drive myself home.

His best friend said, "I don't know what you've done to him, but he is crazy about you. He's not going to let you go or leave you alone. You need to go to the police."

This statement was sobering. They had been friends for probably 40 years. If he was telling me I needed to protect myself, I had to listen.

At the same time, I thought, *'I haven't done anything to this psycho. Why are we women always blamed for the man's crazy behavior?'*

I thought about generational curses. Of how the sins of the father often rest upon the children. The parents' madness can rob the children of their sensibilities. His father had killed his mother in a jealous rage when he was a child. I needed to go to the police.

I filed the report telling them that the bar incident was a carryover from the incident at my home. I showed them the black and blue bruises on my body. They took pictures. I told them about both the excessive alcohol usage and the cocaine. He was a firefighter, in addition to owning his own business, so I was really putting him on blast.

When the police questioned him, he denied being at my home, instead proclaiming to have gone to the motorcycle club upon leaving the club at 2:00 am. on Saturday morning.

His wife refused to collaborate his story stating she didn't know what time he came home on Saturday or where he had been. She indicated that she had been in the club on Sunday but left before the incident.

I sat in the back of the courtroom. I wanted to hear the

outcome of it all, the resolution. He was banned from the club where the incident occurred for a period. He was required to refrain from the use of cocaine. He had to take substance abuse classes or counseling as part of his continued employment with the City Fire Department. He had to serve 30-days community service. He was to stay the hell away from me! Not to call me or have any contact.

It was over.

I was free.

I was at my lowest point.

ROCK BOTTOM

"God is our refuge and strength, an ever-present help in trouble." – Psalm 46:1 NIV

Now What?

"In their hearts humans plan their course, but the Lord establishes their steps." – Proverbs 16:9 NIV

I had escaped permanent entrapment. I survived the physical abuse, but not the mental/emotional onslaught that was ever present, a crippling weight.

Crooked feet. Ha! I had no feet and my legs had gone through the meat grinder. I was in shreds.

I was empty. It felt as if my life had been wasted and was without purpose. Any self-esteem I may have once possessed had been long gone. Yes, my esteem had been eroded. Initially, it was slightly chipped away, but later it was as if chunks fell off, until there was nothing left.

I was still in a state of heartbreak and depression because the one decent man that I loved was not for me. I was too dysfunctional for him to love. Or, maybe he just loved the other woman. They had known each other longer. Perhaps he just chose her and not me. It could have been that simple.

At any rate, I had been in total despair for years. And, it only heightened. I felt hopeless, embarrassed, full of shame, and remorse. I felt used up. Dirty. Empty. It seemed impossible to acquire any semblance of cleanliness or wholeness.

In one sense my mind disconnected from the world regarding their opinions about me. I had to so that I could continue to function. The truth was my own opinion was lower than anything they could fathom.

I did an unconscious reset to automatic pilot and got on with the motions of life. I was working every day. I began picking up pieces of decent parenting and trying to salvage my son's soul.

David Charles is beautiful. He is intelligent and bright, with a quick wit. Also, I see how he is gifted and talented. He has a sensitive soul.

The truth is David also has fissures from my reckless life. He holds these along with his own cracks from the unfortunate trauma he experienced during his young adulthood. This includes the unimaginable loss of a beautiful woman who was shot and killed, sitting in the car next to him, as she tried to drive away from an attempted carjacking.

Remember that Japanese bowl? His fissures and cracks are also painted with gold. He is more unique and will come out stronger from the fire because of them. What were his flaws will be transformed into his super powers. He will make a significant impact on his generation. His spiritual gifts will arise and flourish.

God has assured me that He has him. My hope and prayer are that he not only has a meaningful life, but that he is able to forgive me. I pray that God enables him to love me unconditionally, as I love him. I look for continued healing, reconciliation, peace, and joy between us.

Day In and Day Out

"Yet you do not even know what tomorrow will bring.
What is your life? For you are a mist that appears for a
little while and then vanishes." James 4:14 ESV

I went to work every day. I came home. I rarely went anywhere.
I was downcast, despondent, depressed, and hopeless.

I lay in my bed at night surrounded by the natural darkness
as well as the gloom that had a grip on my soul. The weight of
negative emotions was crushing. It felt so heavy at times that I
didn't know how I could get up and walk, let alone function.

I was tired and weary. I was ready to give up, to call it quits. It
was 1994. The holidays were approaching. I started getting things
in order: all my papers, cleaning the duplex, and organizing.

I thought Mikki would take David if I was gone. It would be
hard on him, but he would probably be better off without me,
given what a broken mess I was.

I didn't want to spoil the holidays for mom. I decided to wait
until after the new year to end my life.

REDEMPTION

PAGE TURNER

"For I consider that the sufferings of this present time are not worth comparing with the glory that is to be revealed to us." – Romans 8:18 ESV

Things in Motion

"Have I not commanded you? Be strong and courageous. Do not be afraid; do not be discouraged, for the Lord your God will be with you wherever you go." – Joshua 1:9 NIV

God was drawing me to Himself. I didn't know it. He allowed me to see it in retrospect. People were praying for me. My mother always prayed for me, but others were praying too. Whenever folks ran into her, out and about, and asked after me she might share that I was struggling depending upon who it was, or just say alright. She would always ask them to pray for me.

She shared with me that one time she was in the checkout lane at the D & W Market in Breton Village. An old friend of hers, who knew me since childhood, came into the store. She saw mom, and greeted her. She asked how I was doing. Mom shared that I was in a difficult season and asked her to keep me in prayer.

The woman turned around to leave. Mom asked her what she was doing, as she didn't go into the store to buy anything. She responded that she didn't know why she was there. She didn't need anything.

She left. She went home and called her family members and friends. She asked them to pray for me.

God had so many people interceding for me. The spiritual warfare for my soul was intense. The demons were pulling out their big guns trying to hold on to me.

Thank God that He begins with the end. I was already His. My name was engraved upon the palm of His hand and written in His book. I just didn't fully realize the depth of all that yet. I didn't know how to truly access it.

So many believers were popping up in my life sharing encouraging words and praying for me.

God reconciled Mikki and me. She was back in church and walking closely with the Lord at this time. She would stop by dropping off gospel music. I would thank her and toss it aside.

My soul had dropped down into a bottomless well. It was impossible for folks to reach me. Impossible for man, but not God. I guess that's why He reminds us in His Word that His arm is not too short to save.

It was Sunday, January 1, 1995. I was home alone. David was at a sleepover with a friend. It was a new year. It would soon be time for me to check out. Perhaps later that month.

I was sitting on the bed. The TV was on but muted. I was on the phone with Charles, David's father. He had been calling periodically trying to stir up my faith.

He was now an ordained pastor, serving at a church in Ohio. God does have a sense of humor. He was reminding me that nothing is hopeless with God. He can turn any situation around. God loves me.

I hear him, but I am shrouded in too much darkness and heaviness to receive encouragement or hope.

"Do you remember what it was like when we first met? How excited you would be to see me? How I would drop whatever I was doing when you came to town? How folks act when they are in love?"

Naturally I didn't care to reminisce over that dysfunction. I didn't want to concede that I had ever loved him. However, after he continued pressing, I relented that I understood his point.

He said something to the effect of us humans having all these emotions towards one another when we are in love.

"If when we love one another, we go out of our way to call and see one another—if we can hardly wait to be together, to catch up, and share ourselves—if we are even willing to sacrifice ourselves—how much more does God want from us?"

That made sense to me. We hung up. I was lost in thought wondering about God loving me and what it might look like for me to respond to that love.

The TV was still on mute. I began scrolling stations to see what was on. In capital letters, it said, TRANSFORMED, on the screen. Remember, it's Sunday.

I turned on the sound. I listened as a preacher spent the next 30 minutes describing me—the state that I am in. It was as if he knew me personally—my beginning, middle, and end.

A New Chapter

"Commit to the Lord whatever your do, and he will establish your plans." – Proverbs 16:3 NIV

I've shared previously that I grew up in the church. I knew that God existed. I had always experienced moments with Him. Yet, I didn't know Him in the manner that I needed. I had called out over the years as I swirled in my dysfunction and disorder. However, I never seemed to deeply connect with Him.

Certainly, His grace was evident, just within the order that did exist in my life, that allowed me to continue working and even to parent at some level.

He kept me and others alive as I drove from the club, in downtown Detroit, back out to the Embassy Suites in Southfield, so inebriated that I couldn't see the white lines on the highway. They were a total blur, moving around. Yet, I slowly inched my way back to the hotel without killing anyone.

However, I never felt like God really heard me, or truly came to my rescue.

The message ended. TRANSFORMED flashed across the screen again.

Yes, Transformed Indeed

"After you have suffered a little while, the God of all grace, who called you to His eternal glory in Christ, will Himself perfect, confirm, strengthen and establish you." – 1 Peter 5:10 NASB

I got down on my knees at the side of my bed. I acknowledged to God that I know He is real.

I confessed my sins, my shame, my frustrations, and weariness.

I acknowledged some of His promises in the Bible that I would like to see manifested in my life. I opened myself completely. I shared dreams and the desires of my heart with Him that I would never speak aloud to people.

I told Him that I have always known He was the one true God; however, I didn't know Him how I needed to know Him. Nor did I know how to live.

I shared that I either needed to really know Him, or I was coming home to Him. I couldn't bear living the way I was any longer.

I reminded Him that in the Bible He promised to order our steps. I promised Him that if He would order my steps, I would follow Him. I told Him that I clearly didn't know how to live, but if He would come and show me, I would live with and for Him my remaining days.

My words can't adequately describe this next part, but I will try.

I felt something warm and gentle, yet significant and forceful, enter me in the region of my belly button. It flowed throughout me overtaking every part of me. It then both filled me within while outwardly encompassing and engulfing me.

It was as if I was being held within a force field, for lack of a better description. Or, as if I was inside a pulsing cocoon.

This was the most wonderful, sweet, good feeling I have ever experienced! It was peaceful and life-giving, strong, and power-ful. It was alive! I could feel its power intensifying such that I became somewhat frightened, even as I knew it was good and would not harm me.

I don't know how long the connection lasted. If it was merely seconds or minutes. I have since had moments with God and been "slain in the Spirit," as they say. I have never felt anything again quite as wonderful as that moment. The power was amazing, unimaginable, and the essence pure and life-giving. I was lost in the feeling even while becoming apprehensive. I inadvertently shifted. My doing so broke the connection.

The first thing I noticed was that the weight that was consis-tently, constantly pressing down on me whether I was awake or sleeping was gone. It had been there for decades. I was so accus-tomed to it that I couldn't believe that it had totally vanished.

There was no heaviness. No darkness. No negative thoughts or feelings. I began searching within myself. I couldn't locate it.

I felt so different. Brand new! So much so that I went into the bathroom to look at myself in the mirror. It sounds silly, I know. Yet, that's how different I felt inside.

I was so changed that I thought it would show in my physical appearance, too. I stood there looking at myself in the mirror, laughing at how ridiculous I was expecting to visually see the difference. I laughed and cried with joy and gratitude that God had touched me. I marveled at the recalibrating nature of awe. I knew that I was going to be fine.

Scripture is indeed true. Old things had passed away. Old emotions, mindsets, and guilt were gone. Behold all things were becoming brand new. I would be transformed by the renewing of my mind. Christ was in me, the hope of glory!

TRULY NEW BEGINNINGS

"I give them eternal life, and they shall never perish; no one will snatch them out of my hand. My Father, who has given them to me, is greater than all; no one can snatch them out of my Father's hand. I and the Father are one." – John 10:28-30 NIV

First Steps

"For those who find me find new life and receive favor from the Lord." – Proverbs 8:35 NIV

I was a new creature. Others might not have known or recognized it immediately, but I knew.

The metamorphosis was both complete spiritually and ongoing in the natural realm. I would work out in my daily life what God had placed within my spirit.

I can't recall the specific order of everything, but here is what began to happen.

First, I knew not only that God loved me, but also that when His Spirit entered me, I was forgiven. Everything I had done, said, left undone, or unspoken was forgiven. Nothing was too dark or horrific, too sullied, or shameful.

I received exactly what the Scripture proclaims that "There is NOW no condemnation for those who are in Christ Jesus," (Romans 8:1). I knew that with every fabric of my being.

Do you realize the freedom that exists in that knowledge? I hope you do. If you don't, know that it is there for the asking. God is no respecter of persons. He desires that we would all come into a saving knowledge of His Son, Jesus Christ.

David and I had begun family counseling for the second time that fall. He shut down and stopped sharing after a couple of months. I continued going, hoping that it would help me, and perhaps I would see an alternative to ending my life.

The therapist highlighted the positive aspects of my life. He tried to assist me in seeing myself more positively by sharing that many of my dysfunctional episodes were related more to the men that I was spending time with than my own choices.

I saw some of what he meant, but didn't totally agree. It was helpful hearing him reframe things and being in the presence of someone who didn't believe I was totally crazy.

I remember our first session after I had been filled with the Holy Spirit. He was baffled. He couldn't explain the difference in me, but he wasn't able to discount it either. I shared what had happened. I'm sure that he was not a Believer. He was confused, without a reference point for what he was seeing in me.

"I would like you to come back for a couple more visits. Just so that we can check in and I can gauge the consistency of your change and behaviors." I said, "Yes, of course. That will be fine."

He told me at the end of the next session that he couldn't make sense of the difference in me, yet it was clearly significant and seemed permanent. He said there was no reason for me to continue seeing him. I thanked him for the time he had spent with David and me.

My prayer has always been that God used this event to draw the therapist into the faith. I pray that he has become a Christian, too.

A Change Has Come Over Me

"Therefore, if anyone is in Christ, the new creation has come:
The old has gone the new is here!"– 2 Corinthians 5:17 NIV

Yes, my experience with the Lord was real. I no longer had a need or desire to self-medicate. That dark, heavy weight truly was gone. My system was cleansed such that it would be a few years before I began drinking socially again. Initially, I couldn't even tolerate Tylenol or ibuprofen. The only drug I continued, at that time, was nicotine. It would be a few more years before God had me stop smoking.

I remember when He told me to quit. I was working as a substitute teacher. I could only smoke before work, my lunch break, and then in the evening after work. This really helped me cut down from smoking a pack of cigarettes a day.

At one point I was only smoking a few cigarettes a day. I was boasting to someone about my progress. I heard just as distinctly within, *"I didn't tell you to cut down. I told you to quit."*

Ok. I set the weekend that Karen and I were going to Perfecting Church's Holy Convocation in Detroit for the first time to finally quit once and for all. I didn't take any cigarettes with me on the road.

Karen was a former BCBSM co-worker, friend, and my next-door neighbor at that time. She was originally from Detroit. She grew up in the Pentecostal church and provided much of my entry into and understanding of the charismatic church, including some of the gifts and movements of the Holy Spirit.

We were at lunch, in-between sessions. I lied and told her I was going to the restroom. Really, I went outside to the car to smoke. I had purchased a new pack of cigarettes at the gas station while filling up the tank.

Karen came out to the car to put me in check. I don't remember what she said, but it was clearly the Lord admonishing me with her voice.

"Ok, then!" I balled up the pack of cigarettes and threw them in the parking lot. God took away my urge and desire for them. He broke my addiction through my obedience.

I remember one time I was having a tantrum with God. I don't recall what I was upset about. Remember, I am just a baby, a newborn in my walk at this point. Anyway, I bought a pack of cigarettes to show Him. I lit up in the car.

Instead, He showed me. It was as if I sucked fire into my mouth! I spit it out. The ash went into the back. I had to pull over on the side of the road to extinguish it. I had to laugh. *'Ok, God, you win. No more tantrums. No more cigarettes.'*

I've been smoke free for 25 years. Thank you, Jesus. Full disclosure, there have been a few more tantrums along the way.

The first week or so after my encounter with the Lord I continued going down to the club out of habit. It had become my pattern. I didn't drink, but the second time I was there I did allow myself to be lured into using cocaine.

I came home remorseful and terrified. I was in such a panic that I couldn't feel any effects of the drug. I had just received the greatest gift of my life and I was fearful that I had discarded it.

I was awake all night. I called in sick to work. I spent the morning crying asking God to forgive me. I begged Him not to take His Spirit from me. He allowed me to suffer a bit before sweetly, with a calming peace, assuring me that He would never leave me.

The point was made and received. I never touched cocaine again. I understood that although I was born again, I still had to learn to live in a world filled with darkness and temptations.

This proved to be true both in the natural world and in my dreams. After experiencing the night terrors following my brother's suicide, it has been rare for me to remember my dreams.

I had one dream that was so vivid it seemed real. It involved me being with a man who was trying to give me to others to do with as they pleased. There was some type of ritual taking place. It dawned on me that I was to be the offering, the sacrifice.

Upon becoming aware of this, a huge portrait that was hanging in the living room came alive. The figure became contorted and evil looking. He began to step out of the picture into the room. He was reaching for me.

In my sleep I began chanting, over and over, *'The blood of Jesus, the blood of Jesus.'* He/It vanished in a mist. I woke up. I thanked God that even in my sleep I was protected.

I went to the club one last time. I was sitting at the bar, not drinking, talking about Jesus and the goodness of the Lord.

The guy next to me asked me why I was there. When I thought about it, I had to honestly respond that I didn't know. It had just become a habit in my life.

He kindly said, "Yes, but that pattern has been broken. You don't belong here anymore unless God sends you out evangelizing." I laughed, thanked him, and went home.

It's a Progression, Just Like Anything Else

"To put off your old self, which belongs to your former manner of life and is corrupt through deceitful desires, and to be renewed in the spirit of your minds, and to put on the new self, created after the likeness of God in true righteousness and holiness." – Ephesians 4:22-24 ESV

It's a process, friends, from glory to glory.

I began reading and studying my Bible again. I spent the first hour in the morning on my knees talking with the Lord.

God had me discard all my lingerie or clothing that was associated with being a loose woman. I threw away all books or movies that were associated with the dark side or horror.

The Holy Spirit would show me artifacts to remove from my

place, presumably because of spirits attached to them and/or what they represented that I was unaware of when I acquired them.

I began watching Christian TV shows, listening more to gospel music. I visited a Christian bookstore for the first time. I would stand in a section and wait to be led by the Spirit to various books.

I was introduced to charismatic, Pentecostal churches and belief systems. I became familiar with the gifts of the Spirit. I found evidence to support some things that I had always known intuitively or experienced.

I participated in prayer groups, Christian conferences, retreats, camp meetings, and Holy Convocation.

I joined Bible Study Fellowship, arguably one of the best studies given its depth in sharing and interpreting Scripture, and comparing both Testaments. I participated on and off for 5 years.

I took classes on spiritual warfare. I underwent deliverance ministry.

Do others need to do all this? Probably not. God will personalize your walk. I'm sharing what I was led to do over the years moving forward to undo the residue from my past and to move freely in the liberty that I was given in Christ.

Revelations

"But when he, the Spirit of truth, comes, he will guide you into all the truth. He will not speak on his own; he will only speak what he hears, and he will tell you what is yet to come." – John 16:13 NIV

There was a dead hibiscus tree in the corner of my bedroom. It had been neglected during my depressive state. There were no flowers. It was dry and withered. I simply had failed to remove it from the room since my awakening.

I was sitting on the bed. God called my attention to the tree, telling me to look closely. There was a brand-new green bud pushing its way up out of a shriveled branch. The tree was dried out. The leaves had fallen off. It appeared to be dead.

God said I was that tree. In the same way I had seemed lifeless and dry, yet there was life deep within that is now beginning to show.

That was such a beautiful, simplistic analogy for me.

God reminded me how I felt growing up in church. Of the time a visiting pastor zeroed in on me, as a pre-teen, asking a question. I was uncomfortable being in the spotlight. He later apologized stating something to the effect that my spiritual aura made him think it would be ok.

We revisited special moments I had experienced with Him over the years. The peacefulness and strength that I absorb from nature. Hearing and feeling music on sacred lands, tapping into the sounds of heaven. The realness of being in thin places, of having knowledge deposited within me, knowing that the wisdom of the ancestors, their connection to Him, and prayers for our family is part of my spiritual DNA.

I was reminded of my delight in being able to participate in the service as a lay reader once I reached the appropriate age! And, of how I reverenced the honor holding it close to my heart, along with the joy I experienced opening God's Word and sharing it with others.

He reminded me how His Word nourishes me and how I come alive when I dive deep in my studies. My participation in various religious study classes were like eating sweet treats or consuming a favorite meal.

We spent several days pursuing this time of recall before He shared that I was chosen to be a minister. I knew clearly that He was stating it, but I had difficulty receiving it.

I grew up in an era when women were not allowed to be pastors. We could lead worship, do committee work, teach, or serve as missionaries or nuns.

I had a heart for those who were lost and disenfranchised,

not only because of my own journey, but also my brother's and father's circumstances. I thought perhaps I would engage in ways that serve these populations. I did. Yet, there was more.

During one of our conversations, I believed that I heard God mention seminary. In 1995, I still had credits hanging out there to complete my undergrad degree. Even so, I went online to search for Bible Colleges or seminaries in the local area.

I stumbled upon Western Theological Seminary in Holland, Michigan which was across the street from Hope College where my brother Bruce had attended, decades prior.

Western had a dual-degree program for social work and divinity. I thought this was a perfect combination for me! Alas, it was full time during the day. I was a single mom, so that wouldn't work. I guessed that I had misheard regarding seminary.

The summer of 2010, I was enrolled at Western Theological Seminary, living in their red bricks townhomes. Fifteen years prior to this, I thought I had heard God mention seminary to me, but it wasn't feasible to attend. Now, many years later, through a series of seemingly random encounters and events, clearly orchestrated by God, I find myself in Holland at the very school I had looked up online in 1995. This was at God's insistence that I move and immerse myself in the culture.

Sometimes there is a waiting period before you see the manifestation of what God has declared. Wait for it!

A CHANGE CAME OVER ME

"See, I am doing a new thing! Now it springs up; do you not perceive it? I am making a way in the wilderness and streams in the wasteland. – Isaiah 43:19 NIV

Living Into the Promise

"Shun youthful passions and pursue righteousness, faith, love, and peace, along with those who call on the Lord from a pure heart." – 2 Timothy 2:22 NRSV

I was attending First Community African Methodist Episcopal (AME) Church that winter of 1995 when I had my conversion experience. I had departed St. Philip's at some point in my twenties so that I could clap my hands and say 'Amen' aloud.

The two churches are around the corner from one another. This was the church that Aunt Edna and her family attended, so I had visited frequently growing up. I knew many of the people who attended. It was a very comfortable transition for me. The rhythm of the service was like what I grew up in without the incense and pageantry.

I was convinced that God called me into ministry. Not knowing any better, or having someone to discuss it with, I shared my call with the pastor. In retrospect, I wish I had waited. Yet, perhaps the timing was more for me to lean into the call than it was for them to recognize it. I knew that I was redeemed, but what about others that knew my past? How would they receive this calling?

I was unaware of the proper protocol, if there was one, and a bit apprehensive. Therefore, I wrote a letter to the pastor and church acknowledging my call. I referenced the Apostle Paul's claim that he was the worst of sinners, stating that I too was the worst of sinners, but God. I shared a bit of my redemptive story. The bishop upon reading it licensed me to preach.

Rev. Parker was shocked by this. He told me, but did not give me the license, or a copy of it. He had a young man that he was walking alongside preparing for ministry. His commitment to me was minimal.

Wonder and Awe

"And amazement seized them all, and they glorified God and were filled with awe, saying, "We have seen extraordinary things today." – Luke 5:26 ESV

I was in a season of mystical encounters. Not knowing any better I would share some of them with Rev. Parker. That is until I told him something one day and his response was "Why would God show you that?

My son was in a period where he was seeing angels. He could see and describe someone's guardian angels. I remember him telling me a certain person had 3 angels. I questioned why he had so many. David replied, "He needs them for protection because of his current lifestyle. God wants to use him later, but he must stay alive to give his life to God."

I confess that I was jealous. I wanted to see an angel, too. I asked God if I could please see my angel. Later that evening as I was asleep in bed, I turned over, opened my eyes for a moment, and my angel was standing there in my bedroom with me! His back was to me and he was looking out the window. I smiled, thanked God, rolled over and went back to sleep.

I shared this with Rev. Parker. "What did the angel tell you?" I responded, "He didn't speak. He was just standing there at the window." He said, "Angels are messengers. If he didn't speak to you, it wasn't an angel." He then stated, "You didn't see that or hear that from God."

I didn't dispute the fact with him. I knew what I saw. I wasn't dreaming or hallucinating.

He was right, the angel didn't speak, but he did bring me a message from God. The message was that angels are real. David really was in a short season of seeing them, for whatever reason.

My angel didn't speak verbally, but he relayed the message from God. His presence in my room acknowledged that God had heard my request to see him and granted it.

This was an excellent lesson early on. One needs to discern when, if, and who, to share the things of God with

This is true even within the church and amongst the pastors and leaders, maybe even more so with them. God was great at encouraging and affirming me, and also confirming what He shared with me.

A.M.E. announced that there was a "Barefoot Prophet" from down South coming to the church. He was Pentecostal, so this was unusual for the church.

I told my friend Karen and asked her if we should go. She said, "Yes. If he is known as 'the barefoot prophet,' he's the real deal."

This was soon after I had announced my call to Rev. Parker and the church. I prayed asking God that if the prophet began sharing words of knowledge or prophesying over people would he please have the man of God speak to me.

I was very specific. I asked that he would single me out and share a word from God with me. And, that there would be a confirmation of my call to preach.

During the service the 'barefoot prophet' acknowledged me exactly in the way I had requested from God. I was called out into the aisle to receive a 'Word.' He knew things that God had spoken to me. He began to say that there would be healing and deliverance in my hands. He corrected himself, stating that it was already there, in my hands.

He then began to lay hands on me, but God prevented him from doing so. He gently caused him to stumble backwards. I believe because that was not part of what I had asked. My request was specific and God answered it precisely so that I would know without question that it was Him.

At one point during the service, I had my eyes closed and my arms outstretched as we were worshiping. I didn't immediately realize that everyone else had sat down. The prophet called out to me proclaiming that I would share God's Word with His people.

Later that summer I spent an amazing week attending Camp Meeting at World Harvest Church in Ohio. Mikki, her mother, her oldest daughter, and I had gone. I can still see the joy on her mother's face as she danced praising the Lord.

R.W. Schambach had just shared the Word of God. He was inviting people up to the altar for prayer or to receive a touch of the anointing. Mikki was encouraging me to go down. She noted that I was curious about being slain in the Spirit since seeing it on Christian TV. She said I needed to go down and experience it for myself.

I did. He shared a brief word of prophecy with me and then laid his hands on me. I immediately went down. Folks working at the altar were trying to get us right back up and move us out of the way because there were so many people.

I couldn't move. The Spirit of God was strong on me. It was different from what I had experienced in my bedroom that day. Rather than consuming my whole being, it was like a fresh, heavy dose. It was powerful. They had to assist me up on my feet and place me in a chair for a moment until I could walk.

I sat for a bit and then decided to make my way back to my seat. The problem was I had no idea where we were sitting. I was as they say 'drunk in the Spirit.' I made my way to the back of the sanctuary and sat on the first row in the overflow section.

Once I realized that I might remain in my present state for a while, I asked God to help me. I began walking down the center aisle again, still clueless as to where our row was. I stopped for a moment. I glanced to my left. There was Mikki. I politely stumbled over folks to my seat.

She said, "Well, now you know it's real." And, laughed with joy. Hours later when that day's session ended, she took the car keys from me. I was still too "caught up in the Spirit" to drive us back to the hotel.

MATURATION

STILL A NAÏVE BABE

Soon after we returned from this Spirit-filled experience, I received a phone call totally out of the blue. I have no idea how Marvin even got my number. Years prior, when I was at U of M, he had been friends with my roommate Robin. She had moved out of state, decades before, once her husband began his medical residency.

He started the conversation by introducing himself and saying something to the effect that he had heard I was in church and walking with the Lord. I acknowledged it was true.

We began talking. He would stop by and watch Christian TV programs with me. I knew that he had a sordid past including violent behaviors. I didn't really take it into account, as I believed that once you truly submit to the Lord you are freed from your past.

This is true. Yet, I was naïve. I was also, unknowingly, ensnared in a false delusion.

Marvin had attended Michigan State University. He was a former policeman. He had a long history of working with disadvantaged youth. He had many positive qualities.

He also, initially unknown to me, was an alcoholic and addict. Or, at the very least, he abused substances. He had a violent history, both within the drug world, with women, and folks in general.

One time he stabbed a guy's hand with a knife at the bar. He had offered him a drink. The guy refused, stating he was getting ready to leave. Marvin felt disrespected. I learned this later, after the fact.

He was working at Kentucky Fried Chicken when I met him. It didn't matter to me. I'm sure a therapist would say I was unconsciously trying to save my brother or father through this relationship.

At any rate, we hung out, talked about the Lord, and after 7 weeks made plans to get married. Yes, you're reading correctly. 7 weeks. I didn't wear a traditional gown, but I did have a horse and carriage.

Naturally my mother had all kinds of red flags. She discouraged me from rushing into this arrangement.

I had asked Marvin what he wanted to do. He liked to paint. Bruce loaned us the money he needed to buy a truck. I got him cards for his painting business. He immediately secured a couple of jobs. One of the jobs was quite significant and lucrative, painting a very large church.

He was living in the basement of the house that his mother had passed on to him. He was renting out the upper units. I had visited the house and encountered a den of evil spirits. I made it clear that I would not live in the house. He would have to move into my duplex with David and me.

We talked about the outreach ministry I wanted to do. He was very supportive of me pursuing it. We calculated his projected income from painting and the rental income; we would be ok if I made less doing ministry.

I was still working at BCBSM. My days as a supervisor had been numbered. I had shown that I wasn't going to kiss up to anyone. I couldn't be trusted from a management perspective.

I can recall Muriel bending over backwards, juggling unrealistic, changing commands in her attempts to please our director, desiring to be recognized and receive further promotion. I wasn't going to succumb to those organizational expectations.

My tenure was too strong and secure to fire me, however, I was given a 'special assignment' while they awaited an opening to place me in the training department. I had zero desire to be confined to a room training new employees.

My ten years came to an end. I quit. I didn't give any notice. I just packed up my personal things one day, left a note, and didn't return.

I didn't tell my family.

A NEW ROLLER COASTER RIDE

"The law of the Lord is perfect, reviving the soul; the testimony of the Lord is sure, making wise the simple." – Psalm 19:17 ESV

We're Spinning

"Be sober-minded; be watchful. Your adversary the devil prowls around like a roaring lion, seeking someone to devour." – 1 Peter 5:8 ESV

I woke up on my wedding day rested, refreshed, with a sharp clarity that had been absent the past 2 months. It was as if a fog had lifted and I could see clearly. I thought, *'Oh my God! I'm not supposed to marry this person.'* Ironically, while attending Camp Meeting at the church in Ohio earlier that spring, I witnessed a singer with a powerful anointing. When he opened his mouth and sang the first note, the Spirit of God flooded the place! I thought, *'God, he knows you. I want my future husband to be a man who knows you closely like this and walks in a powerful anointing.'*

How on earth, only a couple of months later, had I even hooked up with someone who didn't really know God, let alone plan to marry him? What a powerful spirit of deception that had blinded me!

Bruce called to let me know that he was going to swing by to see me. He would be walking me down the aisle giving me away in place of daddy.

He didn't stay long. He just wanted to check on me to make sure I was alright and ready for my big day. I assured him that I was.

My mind was crystal clear. I knew what I was getting ready to do was a massive mistake. Yet, my fear of no longer having my management salary was greater than my fear of marriage.

For whatever reason I had been ensnared in a fog of delusion for 7 weeks. I now would have to bite the bullet and live with the consequences.

Val, Bruce's wife at the time, kept asking me if I wanted her to call it off. She didn't know what I was thinking or feeling, but she apparently sensed something quite strongly.

"Debbie, it's alright. I'll tell Mary. Your mother will be fine. You don't have to go through with this. Folks may go home or everyone can just come and hang out at the venue you booked for your reception. You can even take the carriage ride if you want."

"Val, what are you talking about? Why would I call off my wedding? Everything is fine. What's wrong with you?

She just kept repeating that I didn't have to go through with it.

The music started. The flower girl and ring bearer began walking down the center aisle. Val proceeded behind them. My big brother, looking as handsome as ever, escorted me down to the altar, and the awaiting groom.

I said "I do."

The reception was lovely. The cake was beautiful with roses strewn about. The food was delicious. We were in a venue where folks could wander into another room and secure an alcoholic beverage if they so desired.

Best of all, regardless of what they thought of this hasty union, family and friends were loving and supportive. We laughed, talked, took pictures, and had a great time.

We spent our wedding night downtown in a beautiful suite at the Amway Hotel. We hadn't been in the room very long before everything went sideways and I was reminded of the clarity that morning not to go through with this.

There was a knock on the door. Room service had arrived with a lovely tray of strawberries and chocolates. He also brought a bottle of alcoholic champagne by mistake, rather than non-alcoholic. He apologized, offering to switch it immediately, and Marvin said, "No, we'll keep it. Thanks."

This was immediate confirmation that I had been disobedient. The marriage was going to be a challenge.

An Illusion of Normalcy

"Who is wise and understanding among you? By his good conduct let him show his works in the meekness of wisdom." – James 3:13 ESV

We survived the night. I set aside the disagreement over having alcohol, saving it for another time. We tried to embrace this idea of being married and enjoying one another's presence.

Marvin was a nice, likable person, who possessed a great sense of humor. We had socio-economic and lifestyle differences we would need to adapt to, but that's probably common for others as well.

We set off for an in-state mini honeymoon. We planned to visit family, friends, and places from our childhoods, sharing memories and getting better acquainted with one another.

Marvin really liked and felt comfortable with my brother Bruce. I remember when we arrived at his home. We sat around chatting. Val had offered us cold beverages.

After some time had passed, Marvin inquired, "Bruce, when

are we going to go to your house?" Bruce laughed, "You're at my house." Marvin responded, "This is a White person's house." Bruce laughed again. "Well, you can see that my wife is White. This is where we live."

He chuckled, and told Moe (Marvin's nickname) he would take him to his 'man cave.' Marvin relaxed, feeling more at home in that space.

Bruce and I would laugh about that every now and then when we revisited my time of marriage.

I was working at Mel Trotter Ministries serving folks who came in for food or clothing. I led a Bible study during the lunch hour and a woman's group once a week. I loved it. Marvin was contracting painting jobs and he loved that.

We went to church every Sunday. I was a minister-in-training and sat up on the pulpit with the other clergy.

Rev. Parker and Marvin hit it right off. Marvin secured a painting job at the parsonage. They ate, talked, and enjoyed hanging out together and bonding.

Our day-to-day life was establishing a pattern and rhythm. However, issues began to arise when Marvin wanted to watch TV shows, listen to musical styles, or go places that I no longer shared an interest in and refused to participate.

He was confused. He remembered me from 'back in the day' hanging out in the clubs. He wanted the nice church girl I had become, but he also wanted the wild woman that he had seen in the past.

It was difficult for him to comprehend that she was dead. I wasn't pristine, but I was no longer what he was asking for either. I didn't care to hear a raunchy comedy act at that point; perhaps because my conversion was so new and fresh. I was on a mission to know Jesus and to grow deep in my faith.

Marvin would become angry and frustrated and act out. There were nights that he would go back to his house to sleep. Or, he might hold back the rent money as leverage for a request he was making of me.

His demons were beginning to show themselves. Emotionally I began to unconsciously develop an aversion to him. Subconsciously I was losing any physical attraction to him. He complained that when he reached for me in bed, if I were asleep, I would push him away rather than cuddle up with him.

It wasn't my intent to hurt or disappoint him, but my spirit discerned unattractive elements that I believe it was attempting to protect me from.

OFF THE RAILS

"Create in me a clean heart, O God, and renew a right spirit within me." – Psalm 51:10 ESV

Following Different Voices & Directions

"Ponder the path of thy feet, and let all thy ways be established." – Proverbs 4:26 NKJV

We were on a downward spiral. I knew that it was my fault since I went through with the marriage when God had shown me that I shouldn't.

I also believed that God despised divorce. I would spend hours on my knees in prayer throughout the week. I asked for forgiveness, for mercy, for guidance to be faithful to my husband and the marriage.

It seems the more I prayed the more disgruntled and active the spirits, or negative behavior patterns in Marvin would become.

He would drink. I believe he was using drugs off and on. His whole mindset was so irrational, defensive, inconsistent, and unreasonable it was hard to make any consistent headway.

Typically, when he was upset or displeased with me, which was often, he would just leave.

When he wouldn't leave, I would pull out some of my tapes from the spiritual warfare and deliverance classes I had taken and play them. Marvin would either calm down, or if the spirits in him were extremely agitated, he would take off.

My son liked Marvin and was glad to have a guy around. He was 12 years old at this time. He didn't understand why I couldn't try harder and do things that would make Marvin happy.

I'm not sure how many months we were into the marriage before Marvin took most of his things and went to stay back in the basement at his house.

It couldn't have been too many. We were only married 15 months. I believe we lived together a total of 6 months if you were to string the days and weeks together.

Grace to Make a Change

"And the peace of God, which surpasses all comprehension, will guard your hearts and your minds in Christ Jesus." – Philippians 4:7 ESV

We were coming up on our one-year anniversary. Marvin asked, "Could we please try to make the marriage work? We can both change and work together. I want to move back in." I said, "Yes, we can keep trying to make it work. We can start spending more time together, but I need you to wait before moving back in. I need to see some consistency first."

I came home from work one day and all his things were back in the duplex. It was too soon. We were still exhibiting roller-coaster behaviors. The truth was that without counseling, significant change, or an intervention from God, Marvin was not going to be compatible with me.

As hard as we tried, I wasn't willing or able to deal with the irrationality or outbursts, not after having found true peace walking with the Lord.

Though my son liked him, the long-term impact of this new instability, after finally entering a peaceful phase of life, was not healthy.

I decided to file for divorce. Marvin was adamant that he was not going to leave again. He loved me. He wanted the marriage to work out. After spending a year running back and forth to his old house, now it was impossible to get him to leave.

I came home from Bible Study Fellowship one evening high in the Spirit, in the best of moods. Marvin was sitting on the couch in the living room. As I walked through the front door, I caught a glimpse of him. I noticed his facial distortion and the presence of a spirit, but I ignored it as I walked into the bathroom.

I immediately felt a heavy darkness. He was standing behind me looking demonic. I don't remember what he growled at me. I kicked myself mentally because I had noticed the spirit when I entered and I didn't begin to pray or take authority. I didn't grab a tape to chase it away.

I thought, *'I can't do this anymore. I won't.'* We had moved into the small dining area. He was sitting at the table trying to be calm. I softly apologized to him. "We both know that this marriage isn't going to work. I'm so sorry. It's all my fault. I never should have agreed to marry so quickly. We really are too different as individuals for this to work out."

He responded, "We must keep working at it. It will get better." "No, actually it won't," I said. "I've prayed about it. God has forgiven me. He has given me permission to file for divorce. I need you to get your things and please leave." He refused. He began to get riled up.

Now, although he had a lengthy prior history of being violent, Marvin was never physically threatening towards me. In this moment, it felt like part of him wanted to strike me, but it was clear that he would not cross that threshold with me. His arms were flailing around though and his hand just barely touched across my hair.

This was my out! I snatched it. I said, "You just hit me. You must leave immediately." He responded that I knew he hadn't hit me. This, of course, was true, but I ignored him. I told him that if he didn't leave, I was going to call the police. I picked up the phone.

The police came out. They were very nice and respectful, especially given the foolishness of our mess. The officer told me that there wasn't proof of any violence having occurred. Since we were married, and in our home, there wasn't anything they could do. They couldn't ask him to leave.

One of the officers said if I felt threatened, they could stay while I gathered some things to stay somewhere else for the night.

I thanked him, as I thought to myself, *"Yes, this will help me build a case against Marvin, to get him out."* I packed an overnight bag for myself and David. We got a room at a hotel for the night.

The next day Marvin had gone to work. He had acquired a second job in addition to painting. David was at school. I went downtown to file a restraining order against Marvin to force him out of the duplex since he was refusing to leave. I stretched the truth, or more accurately, I lied and claimed that the brushing of my hair was him trying to strike me.

I truthfully stated that although that had been the first time, given his long history of violence, I was nervous. I shared that he had a tremendous amount of anger and disappointment since I was filing for divorce. I wasn't quite sure what he might do, so I needed him to vacate my premises. He owned a home that he could stay in.

The woman asked me if he had any weapons. I responded, "No. I'm not aware of any." She recognized his name and asked if he was a former policeman. I said, "Yes." She responded, "Then, yes, he has a gun. They all do." She immediately expedited the personal restraining order. He was served later that day at work.

He was so sad and powerless when he came to get his things. I felt guilty, but also that I did not have any other recourse. He moved out. I later discovered that he had taken my wedding dress with him. Much later someone said that they had witnessed him dancing with it in his basement.

We went to court in December. The judge disclosed that he knew Marvin from his time as a police officer. Marvin had been at his home in a social setting for a party. He asked if I was comfortable with him overseeing the case. I replied, "Yes, it's fine."

He asked Marvin if he understood my petition for divorce. He said, "Yes, but I don't want a divorce." The judge said, "Yes, I can appreciate that. She looks like a lovely young lady. However, given that Michigan is a no-fault state, I must grant her petition."

That was that.

MOVING ON

"And we know that in all things God works for the good of those who love him, who have been called according to his purpose." – Romans 8:28 NIV

Next Steps

"For we do not have a high priest who is unable to sympathize with our weaknesses, but one who in every respect has been tempted as we are, yet without sin. Let us then with confidence draw near to the throne of grace, that we may receive mercy and find grace to help in time of need." – Hebrews 4:15-16 ESV

My short marriage had been a mistake from the very beginning. And, I knew it. I felt like I had let God down. I also felt badly for Marvin. He had entered the marriage with good intentions. He had wanted it to work even though it was such a horrible mismatch. I hoped that one day he would be able to forgive me. I also hoped that he gained wisdom and knowledge from the experience as I did.

I was astounded that I didn't feel any disappointment from God. I was so accustomed to my family telling me about all my shortcomings and misgivings rather than celebrating the positive aspects of my life. Disappointment always stoked the fires of guilt and shame preventing them from dying out.

However, God had already taken away my guilt and shame. He never places any on me. Instead, He accepts my confession and my repentance. He convicts me, pointing out when I am wrong and the sin in my life, so that I can repent. He accepts me, always. He uses everything for my good, teaching me each step along the way of our journey.

It was an incredible way to begin living! It is hard. I am not always a good student, but I am faithful and committed.

God knows my sincerity and my heart's desire to be pleasing to Him. He tells me that "I am altogether beautiful" (Song of Solomon 4:7); "the apple of His eye" (Psalm 17:8). God "takes great delight in me and rejoices over me with singing" (Zephaniah 3:17).

I am in the beginning stages of learning to run towards Him rather than away from Him.

He offered me a great lesson in this regard. At one point, after leaving Mel Trotter, I was working overseeing the children at a shelter for abused women. I was responsible for having activities for them during the day.

I did an initial intake assessment on the children to determine if they had been physically or sexually abused. If so, I would schedule an appointment with the therapist at the Children's Center.

I was well-liked and respected by my employer, staff, and the residents.

There was one client who gravitated towards me. She shared that she had escaped from a cult of Satanic worshippers. They had been grooming her as an offering for the leader.

Once when we were talking, she noted how strong the Lord's Spirit is upon me. She warned me though that I was naïve about the power of the enemy and his subtle ways.

I gave her information about the woman I knew doing deliverance ministry. She went to see her. I'm not sure how that went long term. I don't know if she ever got free from the cult. In the short term, it didn't go well. She walked home in the rain. She was not in a good mood.

Someone new had joined the house earlier in the day after my shift. This person embraced her, wrapping around her offering comfort. The influence of this person turned the entire house, residents, and staff against me.

I was called in the next day and dismissed from my position. I was shocked and devastated. Things were just beginning to stabilize a bit financially. Now what would I do?

I knew that the young woman was right. I had underestimated the power and influence of the enemy.

I was bruised terribly by this onslaught that was impossible to see coming. I retreated to lick my wounds. I called Mikki for her support. She was unavailable. I couldn't connect with anyone else either. I felt totally isolated and alone. Abandoned.

It was as though God blocked every other avenue. He wanted me to turn to Him. Within myself I kept hearing 'Thou he slay me, yet will I praise him.' And, each time I would think that's not right. What is it?

Oh, yeah, duh, "Though he slay me, yet will I trust him." God wants me to trust Him. All right, Lord. No matter what, I will purpose to trust you. However, I will need you to help me walk it out.

Facing the Thing I Feared

"With His love, He will calm all your fears." – Zephaniah 3:17 NLT

You may recall that after awakening to the fact that the

marriage was a mistake, I went through with it because I had walked away from my management position at Blue Cross Blue Shield of Michigan. I was terrified of not having a job, even though I had always worked since the time I was 16.

Fear is one of the most powerful weapons in the arsenal of our enemy, Satan. God tells us in His Word that we "do not have a spirit of fear, but rather a spirit of power, love, and a sound mind."

I am now facing that which I feared when the fog dissipated on my wedding day. I didn't have a job with an adequate salary.

The difference was I now had the faith to deal with it that was lacking on that day. My mind was not sound on my wedding day. Yet, God has, and still is, redeeming that time.

It's now been about 17 months since my departure from BCBSM. I had walked away from a decent paying managerial position with full benefits, to do something I loved, but for a meager wage.

I had even begun a second part-time job months before my divorce given how erratic and inconsistent Marvin was contributing towards the household expenses even when we were trying to make a go of the marriage.

I worked the second job for maybe 3 or 4 months. I was on the midnight shift at a residential care home in Sparta.

We were responsible for some light cleaning, prepping breakfast, waking the residents in the morning, doing their personal grooming, and getting them dressed to start their day.

I depended upon God for everything. I asked Him for whatever I needed. I had always experienced a bit of the mystical with Him. My beliefs were even stronger now that I was walking with Him.

I had to assist those who were unable to attend to themselves alone in the bathroom. I helped them to wash up, changed their pads during menstruation, or wiped their rear ends.

I would pray and ask God to not allow me to experience any bad smells or gag while I was assisting them. He answered my prayers every time.

I remembered this many years later when I was in Egypt doing prayer ministry. We went to visit our Coptic Christian sisters in Garbage Village, a slum settlement at the base of Mokattam Hill on the outskirts of Cairo.

There was literally garbage everywhere. There were stalls as large as a 2-car garage filled with trash that people sort through to sell. Their homes, school rooms, and markets were all right next to the garbage.

I remembered my time working in the home. I told God I could do this if I didn't smell the garbage. I also asked that He please keep the flies away from me. He honored my request.

Each time I return to Cairo I ask Francine if we are going to see our friends in the Village. I pray as we approach it, for me not to smell anything, and for God to bless our time together. God always answers that prayer.

One of my ladies at the Sparta home was Carol. She had a wicked sense of humor and was a delight. She was also a very large woman and pretty much dead weight. There was a hoist next to her bed that was used to get her up.

In the mornings, I would pray and ask the angels to help me move her to get her dressed. We would roll her to one side placing her arm and leg in the garment and then roll her back to finish with the other side. An angel would help me lift her enough to pull up her pants. We would then get her into the hoist, at that point I could manipulate placing her in her chair to transport.

Most of you won't believe this. It doesn't matter. It's true whether you believe, or not. God did many sweet generous things with me during my baby-Christian years. He honored my faith, acknowledged, and encouraged the mystical nature He gave me.

CRAWLING BEFORE I WALK

*"The reward of humility and the fear of the Lord are
riches, honor, and life." – Proverbs 22:4 ESV*

Another Fresh Start

*"For freedom Christ has set us free; stand firm therefore, and do
not submit again to a yoke of slavery." – Galatians 5:1 ESV*

That December, David and I had one of our best Christmases
ever! Christmas is my favorite holiday. We had a beautiful tree
that was given to us. We decorated and baked goodies. We had
peace in the house.

My gifts were modest that year. Several had been obtained
from Mel Trotter Ministries. David was ok with that. He and
I volunteered at Degage Ministries and gave out simple gifts of
socks, gloves, personal toiletries, and a treat to those in need. It
was his favorite part of the holiday celebration that year.

We began moving forward. I swallowed my pride and switched
jobs to Kohl's department store. I was hired as a floor supervisor. The reality was except for doing employee scheduling and
some merchandise floor planning, I was just another cashier. I

was embarrassed at first seeing folks that I knew in the store. I swallowed my pride, quickly got over it, and thanked God that I was working.

We barely made it through the year. Once I spent my savings from BCBSM things really got tight financially.

I was still doing Bible study. One of the things that God was teaching and showing me was how faithful He is. I received a notecard in the mail that still sits on my bedroom nightstand. When I opened the envelope a $100 bill fell out.

The quote on the front of the card reads, "The test of a man's vision is what it takes to discourage him." The opposite side shares a Scripture text: "So do not fear, for I am with you; do not be dismayed for I am your God. I will strengthen you and help you; I will uphold you with my righteous right hand," Isaiah 41.10. This Word has been my lifeline these past 25 years.

God continuously shows me His provisions in unexpected ways. One time this manifested as a lesson on Boaz, from the Book of Ruth in the Bible. God showed me what it is like for Him to place a provider in someone's life.

Every month I would get a small stack of white envelopes and write which bill needed to be paid on the front. Every month there would be enough money to pay each bill except for my rent.

I continued to live in the duplex for 6 months without paying rent. The landlord was aware of my divorce and struggle. He and his wife had prayed and offered grace. Here's the kicker though. He contacted me to let me know that he was turning over the handling of his rental properties to a company. I would need to make the June rent. I was scheduled to start a new, decent paying job in June. One month too late. I lost the duplex.

Once again, I had to trust God in a devastating situation. I was going to walk away and just leave everything. Mikki insisted that we pack. She rented a U-Haul and a storage unit for me. David and I moved into my mother's 2-bedroom apartment for a short while.

Prior to losing my place, Renee was calling me and encouraging me to apply for a job at the Grand Rapids Job Corps Center, now Gerald R. Ford Job Corps Center. I didn't know anything about them. She gave me an overview and insisted it would be a good fit for me. I never followed through.

One day, she showed up at my door with an application. She sat down and waited for me to fill it out. She took it, saying that she would submit it for me. I later found out, and told her, that the application period had closed. She said that it didn't matter.

She was right. I received a phone call for an interview. I wore my orangish/red power suit from my BCBSM days. The Residential Director conducted the interview which went very well. This was particularly surprising since I had no idea what positions were open for hire.

At the conclusion of the interview, she asked me which position I was interested in. I politely asked her to remind me of all of them again, please. She noted about three different jobs, one of which was as a residential supervisor. I replied, "Yes, the supervisor position, of course."

The position's schedule was a horrible split shift. I worked the midnight shift Tuesday through Thursday. I got off Friday morning and then returned that afternoon at 3:00 pm. On Saturdays, I worked Noon until 9:00 or 10:00 pm.

More Encouragement

"The grace of the Lord Jesus Christ be with your spirit." – Philemon 1:25 NIV

That May, prior to moving out of the duplex and starting at Job Corps, I went over to Detroit to attend Perfecting Church's Holy Convocation. This is when I quit smoking.

Eventually I began attending church there regularly. I would drive down every Sunday. I attended the morning service, grabbed a bite to eat, and went to the 3pm. service, and drove home.

I did this for two or three years. I even took some of the Job Corps students with me once I started working there. Many of them were from Detroit and would need a good church home once they returned.

Anyway, there was a woman preacher there that weekend. She had a very strong, sweet anointing on her. She loved the Lord. She was a worshiper. After she shared the Word, she began singing and praising God.

She then began speaking forth words of prophecy. When she said, "Your latter years are going to be greater than your former years," my spirit leapt! She told those who were currently struggling that it didn't matter what we were going through because it was temporary.

I knew that this was a Word from God for me. I ran down front and joined the folks dancing without a care. It didn't matter that I didn't have rhythm or what I looked like to others. I knew that was a promise God was going to keep with me. I didn't know about anyone else, but I knew my latter years were going to be greater than all the hell I had experienced. I laughed, cried, praised God, and danced!

SPIRITUAL BOOT CAMP

DARKNESS

*"The light shines in the darkness, and the darkness
has not overcome it." – John 1:5 NIV*

So Many Lessons

*"So that we may no longer be children, tossed to and fro by the
waves and carried about by every wind of doctrine, by human
cunning, by craftiness in deceitful schemes." – Ephesians 4:14 ESV*

My experiences at Job Corps would fill a book in and of
themselves. Director Johnson, who was so warm, friendly, and
gracious hiring me for her department, soon turned coats on me.
This most likely happened due to the influence of Ms. Paris, the
primetime residential supervisor. She and I initially shared her
office which was a long space between the 2 sides of the horseshoe
shaped dormitory.

I hadn't been there long before Ms. Paris began sabotaging me.
She would leave incomplete shift messages, fail to inform me of
major incidents in the dorm, or sometimes not convey changes
in plans from the director. There were times when she wouldn't

leave out the materials that the staff needed on my shift. She would tell lies about me.

I would go home from my shifts and sob. I was confused and distraught. I knew that God had placed me there to work. I would cry out asking Him why He was allowing me to be treated so poorly. He would always respond that He was working on my character.

Sometimes I would think, and even ask, *'Well, what about their lack of character?'* I knew that I was a work in progress, but what about them? He would tell me to pray for my enemies, and to love them.

One time Ms. Paris paid a couple of the students to overturn things in our office and make a mess. She reported to management that I had a fit, suggesting that perhaps I was on drugs, or something. She was hoping I would be reprimanded or fired. It didn't work. We had to go through security entering and departing the Center. The disruption occurred off-shift. I wasn't even on the grounds when it happened.

The outcome of this fiasco benefited me. I was finally given my own office space, a nice big room. There were a couple of times when the shenanigans did work. I was reprimanded twice and required each time to stay home a week without pay. Each time God provided the weekly pay from another source.

One time, a different Residential Director twisted and distorted a misunderstanding to Human Resources because I had offended him by not eating a meal he served.

We had a staff meeting at his home. He offered a meal which I politely refused since I had plans to eat with a friend later. I did nibble and have a beverage trying to be polite because I was aware of his Middle-Eastern customs.

I was sexually harassed by him continuously: flirtation, inappropriate overtures, and lewd comments. Once I had new highlight streaks in my hair, he commented that he liked my hair and wondered if all my hair had new streaks. It took me a moment to realize exactly what he was stating. I was shocked and extremely offended!

I reported him to the Center Director, but they were bar buddies. He blew it off, stating that Mustaf didn't mean any harm.

I eventually reported it to the Human Resource Manager, not knowing that she was having an affair with him. She, of course, didn't pursue any action either.

Later, I wished that I still had a bit of my quick wit from the past. I would have nicely pointed out that he would have to continue wondering about my highlights because he certainly would never know.

I suppose it was good that I wasn't quick anymore. I may have been sent home for another two weeks.

Refuge & Clarity

"When you pass through the waters, I will be with you; and when you pass through the rivers, they will not sweep over you. When you walk through the fire, you will not be burned, the flames will not set you ablaze." – Isaiah 43:2 NIV

One nice thing about working the midnight shift was spending much of the evening studying Scripture, and listening to sermons or gospel music.

Once the staff completed their work assignments some would find a safe place out of sight to sneak a nap, others would read, or work on their own projects, and the residential floors would be peacefully quiet. When I began walking purposefully with the Lord, one of my first assignments was to write down every Scripture text that referenced who I am in Christ, what I have received from Christ, what I can do in Christ, etc. I had pages of these.

God didn't want me to just read them. I learn and remember by writing things down. I brought those pages to work with me and studied them in the quiet of the night once all had settled down.

I had a framed Scripture quotation on the top shelf of the bookcase in my office. "Finally, brothers and sisters, whatever is true, whatever is noble, whatever is right, whatever is pure, whatever is lovely, whatever is admirable – if anything is excellent or praiseworthy – think about such things," Philippians 4:8.

I recall when one of my Residential Advisors noticed it. Barbara glanced between the text and me a couple times before saying, "That is going to be very difficult, if not impossible, for you to do here at this Center." But, for the grace and power of God she would have been right. It required focused intentionality and total reliance on the Holy Spirit.

One time Director Johnson gave me an extra assignment to be completed over the weekend. "McCreary, I need the first floor to be cleaned and mopped (which was something typically performed by the custodial staff), the entire grounds cleared of all trash and the grass mowed."

"Alright," I responded, "we will take care of it after we complete our dorm duties."

"Humph! You don't seem to be bothered by the extra work or have any concerns about getting it all done before the students begin signing out for their day passes or engaging in fun activities."

"Well, ma'am, if that's what we must do today, then so be it. I'll let them know that day passes and recreational activities will be delayed until we get everything accomplished. The students will take care of it. If everyone works together and kicks in it shouldn't take too much time. I'll give them a treat or incentive."

Rather than being glad about my optimism and the anticipated cooperation of the student body, she resented it. "Oh, that's right. I forgot; you walk on water. They'll do anything for you." To which I replied, "I merely respect them and try to meet their needs on Center. They know that I'm here for them. That's all."

At one point she brought in someone from another Center where she had previously worked. She told me that he would be shadowing me on the midnight shift to make suggestions for improvements of our protocols.

He and I hit it off. One evening on our lunch break he shared that she had brought him there to document things I was doing that could possibly result in my termination.

He began criticizing her and our residential and recreation programs. He also started compiling a thesis against her in hopes of garnering her position.

She found out, hurriedly packed him up, and shipped him back home.

Darkness You Can Feel

"to open their eyes so that they may turn from darkness to light and from the dominion of Satan to God, that they may receive forgiveness of sins and an inheritance among those who have been sanctified by faith in Me." – Acts 26:18 NASB

The Job Corp Center was my spiritual boot camp. It was a training ground, a place of learning and putting into practice the knowledge and spiritual insights I was gleaning.

The atmosphere at the Center shifted according to who was in charge. It ebbed and flowed from light to dark, a heavy oppressiveness to a positive openness.

An older gentleman, relatively nice, but passive, was the Center Director when I was hired. He left within my first year being replaced by his much younger Deputy Director.

Director Henry was a mixed bag with some nefarious qualities. If something was happening that he hadn't sanctioned, he knew of it. He either allowed it or squashed it. He had his own "goon squad" to carry out acts of intimidation in the dormitory.

Sometimes there were activities taking place that should have been halted.

He did allow me the freedom to take the students out in the community for various positive activities and events. There were students, both male and female, that attended a play or ballet performance for the first time. It was pure joy watching the guys sitting on the edge of their seats mesmerized by a performance.

He also allowed me to use a Center vehicle on occasion to take some of the students to church in Detroit. We would be gone all day. The students often slept or were quietly reflective on the way down to the city. The gospel music was uplifting and Pastor Winans always shared a deep, meaningful message. Everyone was fully awake and enlivened for the journey back to Grand Rapids. We would stop for dinner on the way home and engage in very personal, deep conversations regarding childhood experiences, faith, and our hopes for the future.

I had much more appreciation for Director Henry following his departure when he was replaced by a bright, mentally deranged Center Director, whose background was working in a prison setting.

Her husband had been murdered answering their door down South, as the perpetrator's act of initiation into a White supremacist group. She carried a lot of baggage and was severely detrimental to the Center. She was eventually fired.

Thankfully, an expert in the field, a man of integrity, was coaxed out of retirement. I was privileged to complete my tenure at the Center under his leadership.

Job Corps is housed in a huge former high school building. There are long corridors, alcoves, hidden corners, an auditorium, a huge kitchen, gymnasium, and recreation area.

At that time the first floor held all the administrative offices and classrooms. The boys' dormitory was on the second floor and the girls were on the third. The girls have since moved into their own building.

If ever two things can be happening simultaneously, the Job

Corps Center totally exemplified this. It serves young people ages 16 to 24. If they can remain focused acquiring the educational and career trade training, job readiness, and social skills offered, they will make significant strides in positioning themselves for a much better future.

The Center had a long, entrenched history of deviant and satanic influence. I was grateful that I had read *This Present Darkness*. It prepared me for the space that I entered.

When I first began on Center the darkness was palatable. When I moved into my own office as a residential supervisor, I could hear and feel the spirits on the east wing of the building.

I remember warning one of the guys that their lair was on that section of the building, down by the auditorium. He recalled this as he was sharing a tale of how following an assembly, as they were putting things away and cleaning up, something just came over everyone. He said he couldn't explain it.

"Ms. M, we had a crazy perverted orgy that no one planned. It was like we weren't ourselves in that moment." He said that afterwards, trying to make sense of it, he remembered my warning.

Years prior to my arrival at the Center, one of the Center Directors kept a female student hostage in her own private dorm room. She could come out for classes. But they say that he had to approve any of her recreational trips or day passes off Center. He monitored where she was going, who she was with, and how long she was away from the Center.

This person had been present at my high school. He had a history of preying on the students at that time, as well, which could be why he left the school district and ended up at Job Corps.

I was told that this girl had a single room, which was unheard of, so that he could visit with her at his whim. She finally escaped and reported him to someone off Center. An investigation ensued. He was removed from his position, but to my understanding, no formal legal charges were made. It was hushed up. He was free to prey on other students in a new venue.

This will sound silly, but at times I felt like the building was trying to kill me. I had at least 5 slip and fall accidents. Now, I am a klutz, but not to that extreme. Two of them were seemingly normal accidents. The most serious one was a student running and accidently knocking me down 2 flights of metal stairs. I was in physical therapy for weeks. The others were just random. I was walking down the hall, slipped on nothing, and I'm down on the floor spread-eagle.

Granted this, and the other incidents, might appear just to be accidents on the surface, but I believe that underneath were spiritual forces in action. And, no, I was not paranoid or delusional. Simply, very spiritually aware of the atmosphere.

Can't We Just Get Along

"If possible, so far as it depends on you, live peaceably with all." – Romans 12:18 ESV

I had several managers which required my adapting to various styles and personality traits.

Once, early into my tenure on Center, I sat in a Residential staff meeting while Ms. Paris attacked me with Director Johnson looking on.

Her onslaught was personal to humiliate me; sharing with others that I had been homeless for a time, which was true. She said that I was back on crack cocaine. I thought, *"I've never used crack. It would be bad enough for you to lie stating that I used the drug, but you are trying to cast me in the worst light exaggerating that I am now back on the drug."*

She berated me in front of the staff for about 30 minutes. I was mortified! I didn't utter a word in my own defense.

Ms. Parker became the Residential Manager during my stint as the Orientation Counselor working with the new students arriving weekly. She seemed to only egg me on at the urging of the current Deputy Center Director, who just happened to be her godmother. This was how she was promoted from counselor to manager without the skill set for the position.

I think she was intimidated by my strengths. I tried to downplay them. I aided her and the department when I could. Yet, because of her insecurities and other forces at play, there were always underlying tensions.

She was fired around the same time as her godmother, who stormed out in such shock and dismay that she left her purse and personal items in the office. Her daughter was sent to retrieve them.

The Center went through a major departmental restructuring which included a managerial position to oversee not only the initial assessment protocols, but the new career preparation classes, in addition to the existing new student protocols.

The residential manager position was eliminated. The residential director would oversee the supervisors in that area.

Parker was replaced by Ms. Jackson in the newly developed position. She was decent. She knew that I had applied for the position and so initially wasn't trusting of me. We worked through that. I knew that she had been handpicked to come to our Center. It wasn't an issue for me.

She was there just over a year before leaving to become a director at another center.

Prior to her departure, she and I did have one major issue when I became sick. I couldn't always work a full day. I would make sure that the basics were covered. She kept badgering me about missing hours. I was eating ibuprofen like it was candy because I was in so much pain. I shouldn't have been working at all, but I was trying to cover things as much as I could.

She blew up one day. My response was to call my doctor who immediately took me off work. I ended up having surgery to correct the medical problem. I was off work for 8 weeks.

Sometimes folks just don't really appreciate you until you're gone for a moment.

Throughout those early years I was mistreated in ways that constituted badgering and/or harassment, yet God discouraged me from trying to defend myself. He was my defense. Many of the personnel throughout the building knew what I had endured over the years. They knew that I was a Believer and was trying to live in a manner that was pleasing to God.

I certainly wasn't perfect; I could be passive aggressive at times, yet, the staff saw how God protected me. They knew that it was His grace and power that allowed me to forgive and purpose to walk in love towards others.

These managers, except for Ms. Jackson, all reported to whomever the current Residential Director happened to be. The last Residential Director, at the time I was promoted to a Senior Manager position, was the infamous Ms. Paris, who had backstabbed and crawled her way into her ultimate promotion.

Surprisingly, after all her hellish behaviors we had formed an amiable working relationship. Others would poke fun at me for being nice and respectful towards her knowing some of the outrageous mean things she had done.

I told them that God had protected me. There were no hard feelings. Ms. Paris is insecure and needs to feel important. I don't. I know who I am in Christ.

She controlled the Center's budget for student supplies and recreation which are funds that I tapped into for the students during their tenure in my area. Though she now continues to harass others, her approach with me is "McCreary, what do you need?" or, "McCreary, I've saved such and such for you. Stop by my office."

All In Due Season

"Therefore, the Lord waits to be gracious to you, and therefore he exalts himself to show mercy to you. For the Lord is a God of justice; blessed are those who wait for him." – Isaiah 30:18

I had acquiesced to others' encouragement and prompting to apply for the new senior manager position even though I knew someone from "the outside" was being brought in.

My friend Karen had been praying as I was going through the application process. She said that God told her I was going to be the ABC Manager. She was making a joke about the long title, Outreach & Admissions/Career Preparation Period Manager (referred to as the CPP Manager). She was really confused when I didn't get the promotion. She knew that she had heard from God.

She was right. It just wasn't time yet. Ms. Jackson eventually left for a promotion at a different Center. I had stopped by to talk with the current Center Director Douglas, the crazy one, to encourage her to consider one of the CPP instructors for the manager position.

She laughed, "There's no way Ms. Tuttle could handle the department. McCreary, what's wrong with you? You're usually sharper than this."

She then asked, "Aren't you going to apply?" I said, "No, I already did, and wasn't selected. Nothing about me has changed."

She looked over at the current Human Resource Manager, not the one who had ignored my harassment complaint. I thought, *"Ah, now you're going to give me the position."* She then said, "It's not a matter of anything about your changing, it's just a matter of timing."

The "word" Karen heard was fulfilled. I joined the ranks of Senior Management!

During the 9 ½- years I worked at the Center I witnessed the terminations of Residential Director Johnson, Counseling

Manager Parker, Deputy Director Jones, and Center Director Douglas. One of my staff also died. At one point, she had stated, "I don't know why folks keep messing with you. Someone is going to end up dead." This occurred shortly after her attack against me, filing an unwarranted complaint with Human Resources, trying to protect herself, which was totally unnecessary.

Residential Supervisor Ms. Paris was promoted to Residential Director, what she had always strived towards, the jewel in her crown, before being terminated. I am not proclaiming that this death and these terminations were directly related to what I endured. I am just sharing what happened. You decide.

Nor do I share this to relish in others' suffering, and certainly not to gloat, only to acknowledge that there is righteousness in the world. It has been a strong reminder to me that God will fight my battles for me, if I take my hands off. He is my rear-guard.

LIGHT

Center Directors

It should come as no surprise that when we had a Center Director that was either a Believer, or a person of integrity, things functioned decently and in order.

There were always those lacking scruples or decency, but their power and influence were lessened when there was someone with morals at the top.

Over the course of time that I was on staff, I saw many more faith-filled folks join the ranks. There was prayer happening all the time. You could feel the shift in the atmosphere on Center as the darkness was pushed back and more light prevailed. Those of us who walked in the light brought light with us.

I can remember one time when my guest speaker for the Women's Day event arrived early and was hanging out in my Orientation room. It was break-time between classroom changes.

A harried looking young man stumbled into the room and sat down in the corner. He didn't say anything. He just sat there. When the bell rang, he got up to go to his next class.

I commented to my guest, "That was strange. He didn't speak or seem to want anything." She replied, "He just needed respite for a moment. The Spirit of Christ is strongly present in the room. He could feel and experience it without necessarily knowing what it was that brought him peace."

The Anointing is tangible. What a privilege to be used by God in this way!

Blessed by Serving

"As each has received a gift, use it to serve one another, as good stewards of God's varied grace."– 1 Peter 4:10 ESV

Yes, there were many challenges, but overall, I loved working at the Center. It allowed me to begin getting on top of things again financially, but also to uncover and use my gifts and talents.

I admired the courage and grit of the young folks' determination to turn their lives around, to position themselves for a better future.

It was both a privilege and a joy to walk with them. They were always coming and going. Each week someone was graduating and new arrivals were coming in on Tuesdays.

Their stories were captivating. Their resilience was inspiring. We encouraged one another by sharing our tales. I was allowed to drop nuggets of wisdom I had gleaned from time to time, and/

or offer suggestions for them to consider as they were struggling with academic assignments or decision-making.

Angela typically had at least one or two nights per week that she couldn't sleep. She would come around to my office, or hunt me down on the floor so that we could talk during my tenure as a residential supervisor. Often, she just wanted something to do.

She became responsible for updating the dormitory bulletin boards. There were boards on each of the six dorm wings that had to be periodically updated based upon varying themes: general information, activities, and multicultural.

She would help plan these. She could change out the three boards on the girls' wings during the night. She had to do the boys' wings during the day before lights out.

She was one of the students who would ride over to Detroit with me for church. They loved getting away from the Center for the day. It was a great time of fellowship. Our conversations were open, non-judgmental, fun, and often enlightening. It was a time when they could relax and let their guard down for a moment, exhale, and breathe, which was significant.

Our weekend shifts were routine. Once the residential advisors assisted the students in making sure that all jobs had been completed, we could chill. Often the staff would get take-out for lunch. Our frequent go-to was Mexican food from the restaurant next door.

The students would request a movie night in the boy's big lounge or a dance party. There was a movie room in the recreation area, but some of them preferred to hang out safely in the dorm. They knew that I would provide snacks. They also knew that if I didn't stay in the room, I was close by. No one had to worry about being bullied or anything going sideways.

I couldn't provide them with as much protection once I switched positions and became the Orientation Counselor.

I remember Ms. Paris thinking I was crazy or stupid, or both.

"McCreary, why are you trying to demote yourself? That doesn't make sense."

"Well, I don't consider it a demotion. It will allow me to work days rather than the split-shift with the midnights. You know I have a son at home. I need to be with him during the evening."

"You'll be overlooked for promotions if you downgrade yourself," she shared.

I said, "I'm not taking a pay cut. I agreed to also handle the multicultural monthly affairs for the Center." She wasn't referring to the pay. I laughed. I reminded her that promotion and increase come from the Lord. I would be fine.

I didn't get to know the students as well in the new position, unless they chose to hang out with me during after school activities.

Hopefully I was helpful starting them out on the right track. I would praise them for deciding to invest in themselves. I would congratulate them for their courage entering the unknown and trusting that they could handle it. I would share pointers with them about Center life.

If their birthday fell during their first week at the Center with me, I would get a cake, and sometimes a little toy gag gift.

I'll never forget one of my tough guys crying when we celebrated with him. He was in his early twenties. He shared that it was the first birthday cake he ever received. He even played with his little toy car. He was another one that went to church on occasion. He introduced me to his dad, who lived in Detroit.

He did well. He enlisted in the Navy when he left. The first few years after his graduation, he would call me every Valentine's Day, which was his birthday, to thank me, and remind me what a difference that validation made in his life. I pray that he is still doing well.

I thrived as the Orientation Counselor. I interacted with and prayed for thousands of students. We admitted between 500 – 600 young folks into the program each year. I held this position for four years.

Granted, most of the students didn't hang out with me after their first week, but many did. All were prayed for continuously.

Many participated in activities that were held on location at the Center, or accompanied me on various off-center excursions. Some of them assisted me with my various projects at the Center, such as planning and implementing the monthly multi-cultural events.

We engaged in conversations about relationships, gender identity, sexual preferences, book or movie topics, career choices, our faith, and even worshiped together.

It was a very rich, vibrant, life-giving time for both the students and myself. In my eyes and heart, and I believe the Lord's, my work at Job Corps was ministry and service.

God continued to use me and other staff members to be light and salt. We encouraged one another, supported each other, and prayed for everyone at the Center.

Degage Ministries

"O Lord, you will ordain peace for us, for you have indeed done for us all our works."– Isaiah 26:12 ESV

I began working part-time at Degage perhaps two years into my position as the Orientation Counselor at Job Corps.

My schedule at Job Corps was Noon – 9:00 pm on Tuesdays for the new arrivals. I would greet them throughout the day as their buses came in from various cities. I hosted an informational dinner with them, introducing them to key Center staff, and then made sure they were settled into their rooms with everything they needed.

Wednesday through Saturday I worked the day shift. So, I was able to begin working a few nights as an Evening Supervisor at Degage.

Degage was started by college students as a coffee house for those who hung out on the streets downtown. It evolved into a full-fledged ministry providing not just food and a place to hang out, but also showers and lockers, an address so that folks could apply for a license or State identification, counseling, programming, and eventually a women's shelter.

Between my two positions I felt that I was living out my calling to ministry. I believed that God had placed me in both positions to serve people.

Degage was a great fit for me. I enjoyed the church groups that brought in the meals to serve folks and hanging out with the clientele. I served as much in the capacity of security as the security guard. Folks liked and respected me so they responded favorably and didn't give me a hard time.

One evening there was a guy hanging out whom I didn't recognize. With an open bottle of liquor in hand, which was prohibited in the dining room, he looked hardcore. I approached him and picked up the bottle from the table.

"What are you doing? Give me my bottle back."

"I really am sorry, but I can't. It's against our policy for you to have it in the dining hall," I replied.

"Ok, ok. I'll put it away and stop drinking. Or, I can just leave. Give me the bottle." "I appreciate that, but policy states I need to confiscate it."

He made it clear that wasn't going to happen. As we were talking, he moved closer to me, and I continuously backed up. I knew that I couldn't return the bottle, as it would send the wrong message to the patrons.

I began silently talking to God, reminding Him that He had placed me there to serve and it was His responsibility to protect me.

While this guy and I continued our verbal exchange and I backed up, another patron came behind him wrapping arms around his waist. "Man, she's just trying to do her job. Come on, leave her alone."

Just like that, he apologized, "I'm sorry." And, he left the building. I never saw him again.

That became a powerful reminder of God's presence and protection in later years when I was traveling around the globe doing ministry.

MAJOR MOVEMENTS

SIDE NOTES

"The Lord will keep you from all harm – he will watch over your life; the Lord will watch over your coming and going both now and forevermore." – Psalm 121:7-8 NIV

David and I stayed at my mother's apartment from June through December 1998 after moving out of the duplex. It was a strain on her. I knew that I needed to be somewhere else by the first of the year.

I had met Ron and Jane at some point during 1997. Mars Hill Church hosted an event with pastor, former professor, author, and lecturer Jack Deere.

Jack spoke a word of healing over me. He turned to walk away, then turned back, and as if surprised, proclaimed, "God is very fond of you."

I remember dwelling on that for weeks, thinking only fondly? Not initially realizing how significant it is for us to be fond of someone or something.

I had picked up a card in the church foyer sharing information about Alpha Prison Ministry. I reached out and met Ron. Mikki and I joined the ministry. We led a Bible study with the women in our local half-way house for a season.

I recall their initial reception towards me being cold and aloof. They thought I was some straight-laced teacher and wondered what I could possibly know about their life struggles. All that changed once I began sharing bits of my own story.

We also struck up a relationship with Jane, Ron's wife. I was to find out that Jane had been praying asking God to send her someone to help at home. I became the answer to that prayer as she and Ron opened their home to David and I for 2 months. I was able to help with cleaning, organizing and overall house-management.

Mikki was friends with a couple who owned rentals. They had a vacant house on Sherman Street with fire damage. Dan said he would begin repairs on the house so that I could move in. The house was slightly crooked. I imagine from buckling under the heat of the fire.

God's presence was so sweet and strong in the crooked house! It felt like home. At one point Mikki, Jane, Jeanne, and I were gathering on Monday nights for prayer. We kept a log of our prayer requests and how God responded.

God brought this back to my recollection this past summer. I accepted His invitation to begin a new Monday evening prayer group with a new circle of women. We met twice per month for a short season. I hosted a 3-day prayer retreat to conclude our time together.

It is reassuring to be reminded of God's faithfulness, and how what He begins, He brings to fruition.

A Significant Personal Shift

"I was with you in weakness and in fear and in much trembling." – 1 Corinthians 2:3 KJV

It is possible to see something, yet place it out of your line of vision. Possible to know something on one level and yet tuck it away, not acknowledging it.

It can happen on a subconscious level when your mind and emotions agree that it's too much. It may be something you don't know how to face. Perhaps you can't begin to imagine how to hold it or handle it. Or, more importantly, you don't want to. It's just too much.

This was the family's posture with our mother's dementia for many years. One of the first presenting symptoms was her incessant talking. I first noticed it when she, Marvin and I went to her favorite restaurant at the time, Thornapple Valley Inn, to celebrate my 40th birthday.

Over the years she began getting lost or turned around when driving at night. We dismissed it as a night vision issue. She always made it home safely. A few times an East Grand Rapids police officer assisted her with directions.

I remember my younger brother joking one time about a car that was ahead of him in traffic. It was moving at a snail's pace. He was murmuring to himself that old folks needed to stay off the road. Once he passed the car, he saw that it was mom.

Her behaviors became increasingly erratic over the years, beginning slowly in 1996 and more dramatically by mid-2004. Again, we noticed them on one level, while disregarding them on another. It was too difficult to imagine or articulate what the symptoms were indicative of and the impending implications.

The summer of 2003 two things occurred, forcing me to take my head out of the sand. I saw Mom come out of the Alger Heights Market looking frantic and appearing to be super-hyper. She didn't know where she had parked the car.

I just stood there watching for a moment, not wanting to acknowledge internally what I was seeing. Finally, I called out to her. "Are you alright? Do you need me to take you home?"

"No," she responded. "I'm fine. I just don't know where I

parked the car." I pointed it out to her. I watched, sadly, as she went on her way.

Later that summer, she was insistent upon having a yard sale. "Debbie, I need to have a big sale and get rid of some things. I can't do it here at the apartment complex, so I will have it on your porch and front yard. It will be great for your neighbors."

I did not want to be bothered with this big project, but eventually I relented. She arrived that morning with two young ladies that I didn't know. They unpacked her car, placing things all over the front yard and my huge porch.

She then proceeded to leave. I was flabbergasted! "Mom, this is your sale. I'm not trying to sit outside all day with this stuff."

She jingles some keys in her hand. "I picked these up somewhere. They're not mine. Maybe when I was at the credit union. I need to backtrack and try to return them."

I finally acknowledged to myself that something is cognitively wrong with my mother. I began mentioning it to my brothers.

Of course, given what she has lived through, finding both a son and her husband dead in the house, it is not surprising that eventually there would be some emotional or cognitive impairment.

We can finally say that aloud, yet are still paralyzed from taking any action, until it all comes to a head. That fall, I received an emergency call from Aunt Edna during the day while working at Job Corps.

"Debbie, Mary's at the house. Something is wrong with her. She's having some kind of breakdown. I need you to come here right away!" Aunt Edna was scared and almost hysterical.

"No, I'm at work. I'm not leaving."

She insisted that I had to. I stood firm, saying, "No. Why don't you call 911 for assistance?" I said.

I felt guilty, yet I didn't feel that I had the strength to walk into another situation like when they called me home for my dad. I was so angry and resentful! I didn't want to do this. Not with mom.

I finally told my manager. "I'm sorry. I have a family emergency. It's my mother. I must leave."

When I got to the Porters' and walked in, I was hit with more guilt. My younger brother, Albert, was standing in the corner, frozen in shock. Aunt Edna had called him when I hadn't responded. He was the least equipped to deal with any difficulty. I felt horrible for allowing him to see mom in that state.

She was not only erratic, but having a psychotic episode. Aunt Edna said that when they sat down at the table to eat, mom just started stuffing food into her mouth.

Mom was hallucinating. She told me that the symbols on the Yellow Pages phone directory had some special significance. Then she turned towards me and said, "I know about the tongues. It's real. You knew all along and didn't tell me."

I replied, "Yes, I know speaking in tongues is real, but I have only recently experienced it. I wasn't keeping it from you."

I move towards her and gently place my arm around her. "Mom, I'm not sure exactly what's happening right now. I need to take you to the emergency room, so they can check you out. Something is not quite right. Maybe we can get some answers. Albert will take your car home." She agreed to go.

There really wasn't much they could do in E.R. We scheduled an appointment for her to see a doctor on Monday. The family agreed that we would take shifts staying with her over the weekend. I took the first overnight shift.

I discovered that mom had all kinds of weird things going on in the rooms that she normally didn't let us go in. "Mom, what's up with all these clothes pins?" They were all over her bedroom and bathroom.

"Don't you worry about that," she responded. "I'm just using them to hold some things together." It was as if they were providing some sort of interference or protection. "What are you doing in my bedroom, anyway? Just come on out of there and close the door behind you."

"Yes, ma'am, I sure will," I thought. I do not have the energy or presence of mind to open that can of worms!

She calmed down from the hyper-frantic state she had been in at Aunt Edna's. Maybe that had tired her out a bit. We talked and hung out somewhat normally. Later that evening, she began making fun of me. She hadn't lost her sense of humor. It was all quite comical to her. "I can see that you're exhausted. You can't go to sleep though until I do since you must watch me."

She laughed. "But, I'm not tired. I'm wide awake," she says, beginning to laugh again. "I wonder how long you will last staying awake." I'm sure that I dozed off at some point. I don't know if she ever did, or not.

I recall my sister-in-law, Edith's, reaction when she arrived that next morning. She looked at me, skimmed the place quickly, noted how hyper mom was, and asked me how long things had been like this. I said, "All night." She responded, "Debbie, you can't do this. We can't do this for the entire weekend."

Her sister was a nurse at our major psychiatric hospital. Edith called her for advice. Helen told her that we needed to do an emergency psychiatric admission which was going to require taking mom back to the emergency room.

I can still see Mom's face peering out from the back of the ambulance looking betrayed and forlorn as they prepared to transfer her from Blodgett Hospital to Pine Rest Psychiatric Hospital. She looked like a helpless little bird. Once again, I was overtaken with guilt.

Not Recognizing the Timeline

"Surely God is my help; the Lord is the one who sustains me." – Psalm 54:4 NIV

Mom was at Pine Rest in the adult/dementia care unit for a

month or so. I remember her being there on Thanksgiving that year. We brought her dinner and flowers that day.

The doctors were able to get her fairly stabilized with medications. We began making plans for her return home. Initially it appeared that she would be able to remain in her apartment with assistance.

While she was in the hospital, Bruce and I had scheduled a hearing to petition for power of attorney over her and what little bit of estate she had. He was responsible for all financial things. I handled all medical matters. Edith's background as a social worker proved helpful to me, as well, discovering resources and moving forward making choices.

Mother was home for Christmas. The first few months went smoothly without any psychotic episodes. She didn't like the fact that she wasn't allowed to drive anymore, but she acquiesced and adjusted. We had the car keys, so it wasn't a choice, merely a matter of mental and emotional acceptance.

The first of the year, something extraordinary began happening with me. I had total peace—every single day. It seemed that it got deeper and stronger as the weeks went by. I didn't know why. It was a reservoir building up for about 6 months.

By the first of March, with Bruce's coaxing, I had decided to purchase a house. Mom couldn't live in the crooked house because of the stairs. I found a cute little house with a fireplace, deck, and a nice backyard in Alger Heights. It was for sale by the owner. My son, David, who was doing real estate by now, drew up the contract and brokered the deal.

I moved in the first of May. Mom was joining me in June. I was scheduled to go to Ghana, Africa on a sister-city 10-year anniversary excursion in August.

While working at Degage, one of the church ladies had told me about the trip. The current mayor and his wife, a group of pastor couples, and a few others were going.

Diane encouraged me to believe in a "Big God," stating that

He would provide a way. She was right! He did. Bruce had tried to dissuade me from going because of Mom's condition. As fate would have it, Mikki offered to stay with her for those 10 days.

Mom was functioning satisfactorily at this time. We had someone checking on her during the day while Mikki was at work. She enjoyed the time with Mikki, reminiscing and sharing great meals.

Experiencing My Homeland

"I thank and praise you, God of my ancestors: You have given me wisdom and power," – Daniel 2:23a NIV

I can appreciate why some people kneel and kiss the ground when they arrive on the African continent. It is as if your soul knows that it is finally home.

We flew into Accra to begin our journey in the Ga District. The tremendous gift of being with the mayor's party on this sister-city excursion was that we were connected to the people on the ground. We were invited into homes and events that I would not have experienced as a regular tourist.

The first thing I noticed was the juxtaposition of the natural poverty and lack against the signage everywhere praising God. Businesses and shops all had signs giving thanks to God and blessing His Name. Hallelujah Barber Shop. Praise the Lord Jewelry shop. The variety of names were astounding!

The people were beautiful! Spirit-filled, gracious, generous, appreciative, and so welcoming as they invited us into their homes and spaces.

We visited one home and were given their guest book. It was their custom to have every first-time visitor sign the book and to write a short note, if you like. It was in some ways a badge of honor for them that God had blessed them with your presence. I was humbled and honored to be able to sign.

We traveled across the Ga District, met with elders, and at one point there was a special ceremony for Mayor Heartwell to make him an honorary chief.

We visited the Black Star Square, W.E.B. DuBois Centre in Accra, Kwame Nkrumah Memorial Park and Mausoleum and Kwame Nkrumah University, among other places. These are all stunningly beautiful, significant tributes to these two men and the freedom movement in Ghana.

The Square was commissioned by Nkrumah, Ghana's first president, to celebrate the nation's independence from Great Britain. The park, mausoleum, and university all honor this great man who led the nation in seeking their freedom.

DuBois, of Haitian descent, was one of the greatest Black scholars and intellectuals in America. He was involved with the Niagara Movement in 1905, a gathering of the prominent Black scholars and intellectuals of the day who were working towards freedom and equity for people of color. DuBois moved to Ghana in 1961. He served as the Director of the Encyclopedia African Project and a Fellow at the Academy of Arts and Sciences.

These two men are giants in the Pan-African movement for the freedom of Black and Brown people around the world.

We attended an outdoor worship service that lasted for several hours. The music, prayers, and spoken Word were very moving. At one point I began looking around to see if there might be a building with a restroom or an outhouse nearby. I finally asked someone, who pointed me towards a small covered pavilion in the back. I approached thinking that it was an outhouse. When I entered, I discovered a slanted cement floor with a hole in the middle.

I was wearing a skirt down to my ankles. My first thought was, *"So God, you're removing my privilege for a moment and allowing me to see how many of your children in the world live. Ok. Well, please help me not wet the hem of my skirt."* Lastly, I asked, *"Could this please just be a one-time experience?"* He was gracious. It was. It put things into a perspective that I have not forgotten.

We went up the western coast to visit Elmina and Cape Coast Castles. There were little children everywhere begging for money. I didn't have any to give them, but I had pieces of candy which they thanked me for.

We toured the castles. We went into the holding room of the larger one. Someone pointed out that the chapel, the sanctuary, was directly above the holding room. Individuals were praying, preaching, and praising God while below them they were holding God's people, His creation, as if they were chattel.

We went into the holding room. We saw the door that they passed through to board the ship, realizing that it was the last time they would see their homeland. We were told that they would have been packed into the large room. We knew that they would be stacked onto the boat like sardines.

The room was like the ship in that there was no provision made for people to urinate, defecate, or clean themselves. If they were menstruating or sick, they would bleed and vomit on themselves and others.

The anguish, pain, despair, and heartbreak of the ancestors' spirits was palatable. I was overwhelmed with remorse, sorrow, anger, and began to feel physically sick. I ran out of the room.

Several of the people in my group came to check on me and comfort me. At that moment, I needed not to speak or be touched by a White person. Just for a few minutes while I held and processed what their ancestors had done to mine.

Time Was Fast Approaching

"a time to be born, and a time to die;" – Ecclesiastes 3:2a NIV

I returned home to mom, grateful for my time in Africa. I remember being in the kitchen one Saturday morning. It was blue, sunny yellow and white. In some ways it reminded me of our kitchen on Bates Street. Mom commented, "You seem to be in a good mood every day. You feel lighthearted. You're always smiling and cheerful." I'm sure she was recalling how years prior I circled in and out of despair.

I responded, "Yes, it's such a blessing. I am peaceful every day. It's such a great gift from God." At this time, I was moving with an excess of grace, peace, and strength that God had built up in me. I didn't know it, but I was functioning in the overflow, and I would soon expend it all.

When I was looking for a house, we both liked the one that we moved into. Mom had a huge bedroom with all of her things. The dining room was turned into her sitting/TV room with her familiar living room furniture and personal items.

In retrospect, I can remember her saying it was all fine, that she wasn't going to be there long. At the time her comment didn't register with me.

There had been one major warning sign as we were moving in, but like with the beginning signs of her dementia, my mind ignored it, tucking it away.

Initially, I could serve her breakfast, leave lunch for her to warm up, and call to check on her during the day. She had a panic button that I insisted she wear just in case she slipped or anything happened.

I also had a baby monitor in her bedroom with the receiver next to my bed. I could hear her breathing in her room. I would know if she fell out of the bed or cried out during the night.

One Saturday morning she climbed up the stairs to my loft bedroom. I didn't hear her on the carpeting, but I could feel someone in the room. I opened my eyes. She was standing next to the bed peering down at me. "Debbie, you're going to be late for work." I smiled. "No, it's the weekend. Thanks for looking out for me though."

I told my friend Karen about it. She recalled the time when David and I had stayed with mom in her apartment years prior.

Karen was living in the apartment complex next door to her. I had come running to her place, pounding on the door with tears streaming down my face, gasping for breath. My mother had said something cruel and mean to me. It felt like she had pierced my heart with a knife.

Karen reminded me of this and then asked, "Aren't you afraid to sleep in the house with her? Don't you think you should have a lock on the door coming upstairs?" I said, "No! My mother would never physically hurt me." Occasionally, after she had planted that seed in my mind, I would briefly wonder. Then I would think, *"Nah, God would never let that happen."*

As the months passed her health declined and became less consistent. I hired someone to stay with her throughout the day while I was at work.

I remember coming home one day from work and she was still in bed. Her caregiver noted that mom didn't feel like getting up, so they had a picnic in bed, and shared stories. God was so faithful, providing the most wonderful person to care for her.

She was in and out of the hospital a couple of times. Perhaps the doctors told me in their medical garble, but I don't think so—no one ever flat out said that she was dying, or gave me a timeline. My own eyes and mind were unable to perceive it.

She had another psychotic episode one time while in the hospital. I came by to see her after work. "Debbie, what are you doing here at school," she asked. "Where are you mom?" "Well, I'm here at Lincoln. You stopped by so you must know where we are." "Yes, I do, but you're not at school. You're in the hospital."

"Well, that's ridiculous," she said. I pointed to the stand holding her IV drip and asked her what it was. "A lamp," she responded. We did this with a couple of items. She identified them as things in the classroom as well.

I switched gears and said, "Well, I hope you've been having a good day." They switched her meds and she came back home with me.

One day she got up to use the bathroom. I wondered what was taking so long. "Are you ok in there?" I inquired. I went to the bathroom to see. She was sitting in the tub filled with water. She had defecated there rather than using the toilet.

I gently held her and my emotions, while wiping her off, closed the toilet seat and placed a towel for her to sit on. I cleaned and sanitized the tub. I wiped her down with a soapy cloth while running a clean tub of water with sweet bath salts. I proceeded to gently bathe and rinse her. I tenderly dried her off with one of the huge, soft towels she liked.

All the while I was comforting and reassuring her, and myself, saying that we were alright. She didn't need to apologize. And, we were going to be ok. As I heard myself, I thought, *"You need to repeat this to yourself over and over again like a mantra if you want to make it through this."*

Soon after, on a day when she seemed fine, she tried to get up, but couldn't stand. I called David. He came, lifted her, carried her into the bedroom, and gently, lovingly placed her on the bed, as tears rolled slowly down his face.

Bruce had abandoned me shortly after I moved into the house. Val had filed for divorce, again. He went into isolation. Steve, Edith, and I talked about options. We decided on a place for Mom's care. She was only there for perhaps two weeks.

Early the Sunday morning before Christmas I received a phone call that she had transitioned in her sleep. I regretted that I hadn't hired 24-hour care and let her remain home with me.

Even as we moved her into the assisted living facility, I didn't know about the others, but I was still in denial, blind to the reality that she would soon be transitioning. She had walked into the facility still mentally alert and conversational. By the end of the first week, she was drugged and looking comatose. I asked to have her transported back to the house. They stated it would be too harmful for her. She was gone the next week.

Had I known that she only had months to live I would have

moved into her apartment with her rather than purchasing a house that I couldn't afford by myself. I stayed there a couple more years before moving out.

I had to laugh. In 1998 when I was being evicted from the duplex, I had been attending prayer meetings and conferences with Minister Walker. I had asked her to pray about my situation, that God would provide a way for me to stay in the duplex.

She told me that moving from the duplex was one of two times I would be forced to move. I remembered this as I was packing up the house. It gave me a sense of peace, contentment, and trust.

I packed, moved out, and stayed with a friend for several weeks until I found an apartment. I began the process of letting go of my regrets and thanking God for His grace.

I was grateful that Mom and I had shared a new space, free of the past and lingering ghosts. One that didn't hold any old memories, as she lived out her last months.

I now knew why God had filled me up for 6 months with His grace and peace. My emotional energy would be slowly depleted as I watched her decline. I would use all my physical and mental energy to manage the day-in, day-out pieces of caring for her. It took everything within me to hold what was transpiring while making sure that she had everything she needed—that she was comfortable, and at peace.

Afterwards, the only regrets were not keeping her home with around the clock care and that I hadn't spent as much time as I should have with her just sitting telling stories and reminiscing.

She knew when we moved into the house that her days were numbered. I believe that she was at peace. She had lived a life of joy, giving, and sharing, experiencing the world around her, and filled with significant friendships.

She had left her mark on her church community, Wurzburg's, the various schools where she taught, and all the civic and social organizations that she had been a part of throughout the city.

She was filled with life while holding the deepest pain and loss that one can imagine.

Her wedding band was still on her finger 25 years after her husband's death. I had it enlarged. I wear it on my left thumb, every day, in honor of them, and remembrance of her.

Returning to the Light

"Arise, shine for your light has come, and the glory of the Lord rises upon you." – Isaiah 60:1 NIV

Weeks before mom transitioned to the Lord, I interviewed and was offered the Senior Manager position at Job Corps. I was the new Outreach & Admissions/Career Preparation Period Manager.

My friend, Karen, had indeed heard from the Lord that I was going to be the "ABC Manager," as she called it. We just had to wait a couple of years for it to manifest.

Mom had shared one of my major milestones, back in 1996, being present when I preached my first sermon after serving a year as a minister-in- training at church. Now I was able to tell her of this significant promotion and celebrate the good news with her. I was glad that she was able to witness this accomplishment, along with me finally securing my Bachelor of Arts degree prior to her decline and demise.

She and Mikki had hosted a wonderful, surprise gathering at her apartment clubhouse when I finally graduated in 2002.

Initially, I was hesitant to interview for the manager's spot again in 2004, as I enjoyed being with the new in-coming students. One of my peers encouraged me, telling me that I would be able to influence their first 90-days in the program rather than just one week. He said that my personality and values would permeate the entire department. That was the deciding factor for me.

Crazy Ms. Douglas, the Center Director, would soon be terminated and replaced by Mr. Henry, and Mr. Rob would be promoted to a director's position. Both were men of integrity. The Center then functioned at its highest level since I had arrived.

It was like night and day for me. I was treated with high regard. My opinions were valued. The light that was present on Center was pushing back the darkness. Staff were able to excel. Those who were not performing well were disciplined or terminated.

Yet, about 6 months into my new position, I knew that it was temporary. I was aware that God was positioning me for transition. I just didn't know when or to what.

At the beginning of my second year in the new position both my Corporate Director and the Corporate Owner began considering me for a higher promotion. I listened to their encouragement and even went through some conversations preparing me for the interview, but I knew that God had something else in mind. God blocked anything from happening. He let me know that the purpose behind their considering me was for me to think more highly about myself, to have more confidence, and to desire more.

The one thing that kept presenting itself to me was school. I had told myself once I completed my Bachelor's degree that I would never go back to school. God doesn't really care about those short-sighted promises we make to ourselves. Or, rather, He may care, but they don't override His plans.

One day the instructor, who had encouraged me to apply for the manager position, came into my office and handed me a piece of paper.

"Read this McCreary. Don't just toss it aside." I assured him that I would. Since I had given my word, I did read it. He knew me. If he hadn't solicited my promise, as soon as I saw that it was describing a graduate program at Western Michigan University, I would have ditched it.

I began to get excited as I read the program description. It was preparation to become a Family Life Educator which also included all the pieces needed to begin and run a non-profit. I thought it might be the closest I would get to starting a nonprofit ministry and more fully completing the Call to Ministry that I believed was on my life.

I prayed. *"God if this is your invitation, please make it clear, and I will accept it."* I reminded Him, as if He didn't already know, that I didn't have any money to pay for school, and I couldn't do it in my current position at Job Corps as a Senior Manager working 50+ hours per week and being on-call 24/7.

My sister-in-law, Edith, mentioned the Thurgood Marshall Fellowship Award. I applied. I was granted an award that would cover two-thirds of my tuition.

I prayed again, asking God to show me where I could work with the flexibility to handle being in school full-time. I was old school; at that time, you could still look in the Sunday newspaper. I saw the perfect position, Education Coordinator for the residential students at St. John's Home, a placement center for abused and neglected children.

When I stepped out of my car onto the grounds for my interview, I heard a Christian song in my head. I knew that the position was mine. The interview went very well.

A week or so later, the Vice-President at St. John's Home phoned me. "Ms. McCreary, we would like to invite you back for a second-round interview; however, I first need to inform you that we are not able to come anywhere close to matching what your current salary must be."

"Yes, I was aware of that when I applied. What other benefits do you have?"

"What are you looking for?"

"I'm seeking a less demanding, more flexible position so that I can return to school. I plan to enter a Master's Program at WMU. I'm wondering if St. John's offers any tuition reimbursement."

"Absolutely. We can cover one-third of your tuition, along with your books, and supplies."

I responded that I would love to be scheduled for the next interview. I was offered the position. The VP had spoken out of turn offering me the educational benefits. They honored his commitment to cover the tuition, but were unable to pay for my books and supplies. I followed God's lead and He arranged for my tuition to be paid in full.

Soon after, I learned that my program required an internship in my department. My Department Chair informed me that they were waiting on a grant and that I could not start serving until it was received. Since this wasn't my fault, they would still be giving me my monthly stipend. The stipend equaled the amount of the pay cut I had taken moving from Job Corps to St. John's. I had been totally unaware of the internship and stipend. I had trusted God and stepped out in faith where and how He was leading me. My obedience was rewarded.

Although I was a Senior Manager at Job Corps, if I stepped away from the Center, even for just a moment, I had to inform them that I was "off-Center."

My new position had me all over the city at various schools working as an advocate for our students. I loved the freedom of moving about!

I began in the summer when there wasn't very much to do once I became familiar with the various aspects of the job. I would ask my supervisor for additional work and/or inform her when I left the building. She finally told me to stop. "Deborah, this position requires you to be off-site. You don't need to check in." She then said, "It's summer. It will be slow until you start gearing up for our residents' school enrollments in the fall. I thought you were in school. Don't you have some reading to do or papers you can be working on when things are slow?"

This was such a contrast to the environment that I had come from that I was initially uncomfortable with the freedom. Once I settled into it, I shared with God that I didn't think I could ever work confined to an office or building again. He let me know that I never would be.

I knew that God had placed me there so that I could attend graduate school. I didn't know that when school was over the position would be too. It took me 15 months, attending full-time, to complete my program with honors. During this period St. John's Home was going under financially. They had begun terminating any ancillary staff they could spare, including the cook and receptionist. My co-workers thought I was safe since I was the only one doing my work with the youth and the schools. They were wrong.

In April, the day before my graduation, I was informed that my position was going to be eliminated at the end of May. I inquired if I was still eligible to use the week vacation that I still had on the books. I was told yes, go ahead, schedule a week if I like.

I laughed when I got home. I knew that God had placed me there for school. I didn't realize that when school was finished the position would be too.

One of my favorite places to be is by the water. At that time, I could book a condo for just under $200 per week using my Star credits with my travel plan. I suggested to God that we should discuss this change of events on the beach. I booked a spot down in Florida. I also told Him I would look in the Sunday paper for a new position. I asked Him to show me where we were going next.

There was an ad for a one-year contractual position, a pilot program working with family caregivers tending children under the age of 5. I applied and headed down to Florida. While there, I received a phone call inviting me to an interview which I scheduled for the following week.

Jennifer was hiring 4 coaches to participate in a pilot program for Early Learning Interventions through Kent Regional 4-C. The program targeted 4- and 5-year-olds who were not yet in kindergarten and their family caregivers, mostly grandmothers or aunts. It included weekly in-home environmental assessments, lessons, and modeling reading/play interactions; as well as weekly playgroups that were designed to hone fine motor skills and prepare the youngsters to begin reading.

I was still in a transition phase. In 2006, I became aware that God was shifting my life; it had begun with my transition to St. John's Home in 2007, and was still in motion. I was somewhat weak with the young child experience, but very strong working with families. She coaxed me during the interview to pull out my family life training from birth to death, my substitute teaching experience in elementary schools, overseeing the elementary students at St. John's, and other previous experiences. I was hired.

While I was still at St. John's Home, I attended the Women's Expo at DeVos Place that March. I had a yearly tradition of taking several of the young ladies from Job Corps. I went by myself that year.

There was a booth offering a hand exfoliating treatment which I tried. The young lady was recruiting beauty consultants for at-home spa events. This was totally out of my foray, but for whatever reason I let her talk me into trying it. I loved it! I enjoyed pampering the women and sharing with them. It was a great side hustle, as you made your money on the spot.

I continued to do this evenings and weekends while working my new family coach position. I was able to hold spas later while in transition, back in school, and during both of my internships.

I was still in a transition phase. The shift that I became aware of beginning back in 2006, which manifested with my transition to St. John's Home in 2007, was still in motion.

It is now 2009. God had let me know that I would never seek employment again. I would go through man's process of applying, but He would present everything. I wouldn't need to search. This had begun with my placement at Job Corps back in 1998 with Renee bringing me the application and submitting it for me.

Now I won't even need to look in any more newspapers. God is making it crystal clear to me that this is how we will proceed going forward. He will present the open door. All I must do is walk through it!

One Saturday in August, Grace for the Nations Church hosted an outdoor event for an assortment of vendors. I registered for a booth to present my BeautiControl Spa business. It was a perfect opportunity to schedule spas and perhaps recruit.

There just so happened to be a booth close to mine sharing information about a reentry house and program for women returning to the community from prison. My research project and proposal for my graduate studies was on women in prison and reentry. My partner and I designed the programming and proposal for a home. Of course, I went over to look at this display.

Patricia and I began a long conversation about not only the women, but ministry in general. I shared the outreach ministries that I have been involved with and being a minister-in-training at church.

"Have you considered going to seminary?" she asked.

"Yes, many years ago, but at the time I was a working single mom. I wouldn't have been able to manage juggling a full-time night job and attending school during the day. As I've gotten older, I haven't given it any thought."

She proceeds to share some highlights about her seminary experience, including the doors that it opened. "May I have the admission guy from seminary reach out to you?"

"Sure," I replied. This was in August.

It was now December, 2009. I was working at home doing my reports when the phone rang. It is Matt calling from Western Theological Seminary in Holland – the school I had looked up online in 1995.

"Hello, Deborah. This is Matt calling from Western Seminary. Patricia shared your information with me. I know it's short no- tice, but I'm wondering if it might be possible for you to come over this week for a tour. I would like you to meet some people before they begin their Christmas break." I said, "Yes."

I drove up to the campus, parked, stepped out of the car, and immediately I heard a gospel song in my head—excitement and anticipation began to stir within! We talk, tour the campus, I meet folks, and receive an application kit, including forms to apply for financial aid.

Mid-January, Matt called to let me know that I've been accepted. I'm thinking that I can begin that spring. He says, "No. You have to wait until fall."

I was disappointed. "Oh, well, maybe I was wrong about God wanting me to go there."

He replied, "God isn't saying no, just that you must wait. Financial aid packages are processed and applied beginning with the fall term in September."

God told me to move to Holland and immerse myself. I didn't want to live in Holland, but I was obedient. The red-bricks, as the townhouses are called, are across the street from the academic building. I had a 2 bedroom, 1 ½ baths, with an upstairs, downstairs, and basement which was perfect for my grandkids to be able to come and visit.

The yearly pilot position with Kent Regional 4-C was extended for about 3 months to complete all the necessary backend assessments. By the time I was wrapping up, God had relocated me to Holland. It was either June or July. I started classes that September.

I believe my graduate program was a means to an end to let me know that I was not too old to attend and succeed in seminary.

I remember when I shared with my home church that I had been accepted at seminary. By then, I was attending a non-denominational church, with A.M.E. roots. My pastor was very positive and encouraging.

One of the other ministers asked why I was going there instead of the cohort program that several of the minsters of color were attending at Grand Rapids Theological Seminary. I responded that God didn't tell me to go to that one. He seemed to have an attitude with me. "You know the curriculum at the school in Holland is going to be very rigorous." I'm wondering what his issue is. I'm thinking, *"Well if that's the case, since you have your degree, why aren't you offering to help me?"* Finally, I responded, "That's probably why God just had me complete a Master's program at WMU summa cum laude to get me ready." I walked away.

He wasn't the only one who took issue with me going over to Holland. It seems some were thinking that I thought I was better than others. The thought never crossed my mind. I was being obedient to the Lord.

A DIFFERENT WORLD

A DIFFERENT KIND OF
INSTRUCTION

"Apply your heart to instruction and your ear to
words of knowledge." – Proverbs 23:12 NIV

I was at a disadvantage with much of the student body with regards to not having matriculated through the Christian Reformed general education or undergraduate schools experience. I didn't possess the familiarity with Reformed theology and doctrines to the extent that they did. However, I did have the advantage of being more mature and much brighter than many of my classmates.

I remember receiving one of my initial papers back with red marks on it though, along with comments. I think I received a B-. I was initially shocked and upset. I wasn't accustomed to this. I gave the comments appropriate consideration, analyzing what my deficiencies were. I immediately realized that I could not give personal responses in the way that I may have done with an organized Bible study. Secondly, I noted that my writing style would also need to deviate somewhat from my social science training. It took me a couple of weeks to get the hang of it.

I didn't complete my 3-year seminary degree Summa Cum

Laude, as I did my first Master of Arts degree, but I did achieve Magna Cum Laude status.

Let me begin by stating that I am forever grateful to the school, the professors, and my classmates that I engaged with for my experience.

Yet, although I had an inkling what type of environment the Lord had thrust me into, the degree of religious superiority that the Reformed Church holds regarding themselves, coupled with how racist and misogynistic the environment was, far surpassed my imaginings.

Most of the students came from small, closed, super-conservative towns and cultures. Many of them had no, or limited, cross-cultural relationships or experience. They grow up indoctrinated with privilege and a false superiority.

I even experienced this playing out in my preaching class between two instructors; one White, Reformed professor, the other Black, and either from a Baptist or Pentecostal background. Their theological variances would become apparent with the White professor demeaning his colleague in front of the class.

Thank God the seminary partnered with the Seminary Consortium for Urban Pastoral Education in Chicago and arranged a weekend housing option for us with McCormick Theological Seminary.

Mind you, ignorance is always present everywhere, but it wasn't as intense and constant as what I experienced in Holland.

I don't recall which class I was attending one Saturday in Chicago, or even what topic we were discussing. What I do remember is my comments being dismissed and/or challenged during our morning session. We took a break for lunch. I decided that I would be silent the remainder of the day.

After lunch, one of the young men in our group, who happened to be White, and had years of experience serving as a Peacemaker in either Central or South America, resumed the morning conversation. He rephrased everything I had shared that morning. Everyone was leaning in and agreeing with his points. When he finished, he told the group that he had just repeated everything that I had shared with them that morning. He noted that their bias and prejudice had not allowed them to receive the information from an older, Black woman.

It was so powerful! I have never had a member of dominant culture stand up in such a way before, nor have I since. It was very encouraging, particularly given the assignment that God was holding for my immediate future.

My ability to be present with a diverse group of various ages, ethnicities and backgrounds in Chicago helped me to maintain my positive equilibrium. I took the maximum number of credits allowed, which I believe may have been 5 or 6 classes. It was enough each semester to keep me refreshed, as well as securing certification in their Graduate Theological Studies Program for Urban Ministry.

Surprising Blessings

"Whoever gives thought to the word will discover good, and blessed is he who trusts in the Lord." – Proverbs 16:20 ESV

I still look back and marvel at the unexpected experiences and opportunities that were afforded me during my time in seminary.

My class cultural immersion trip took place in January 2011. We traveled to Chiapas, Mexico. We learned about the RCA mission work in the country, the blending of Christianity, Catholicism, and native religions.

We learned some of the history of the Zapatista uprising, the fight of the indigenous people to maintain their freedom, culture, and livelihood. I was surprisingly invited to speak to the women in one of the villages we visited.

We spent a night in the home of one of the locals. I recall

waking up in the middle of the night wet. I looked around knowing that it wasn't raining, wondering what could possibly be leaking. We were all in one room separated by sheets that were hanging to provide a partition between us. I was trying to be quiet as I stumbled around in the dark for dry clothes.

I discovered that the blanket I was given was still damp. My first reaction was a feeling of whining and complaining, the negative reaction birthed from my own privilege and material comfort. I immediately felt convicted and confessed. I looked over at the small vase with a flower that my hostess had placed by my bed. I realized that in addition to that sweet touch and sweeping the hut; she had also washed the blanket preparing it for her guest. She had been thoughtful, generous, and kind with the little that she had.

I thought I was advanced in my ability to adapt well in a variety of places and circumstances and to a large degree, back at home, this was true. I was discovering that what I considered lack and difficulty at home was far surpassed by the challenges in developing countries. I, of course, knew this intellectually. I was now experiencing it first-hand which was one of the reasons for the excursion.

That spring, a small class cohort traveled down to Lindenwood Spiritual Retreat Center in Indiana to explore spiritual disciplines.

I encountered the sweet presence of the Lord's Spirit when we came on the grounds. The time of self-reflection and exploration was profound. The experience caused me to let my guard down and begin engaging more fully with my peers.

I was chatting with Matt as we headed back to our vehicle from a restaurant. He mentioned that he was beginning to work on scheduling students' summer internships. "I'm thinking about where to place you."

I responded, "I thought that didn't happen until after our second year." "Yes," he said, "That normally is the schedule, but since you're older with so much outreach ministry experience, as well as another graduate degree, I'm going to schedule you for this summer."

He then inquired, "What would you think about going down to St. Thomas." I'm thinking, *"The island? And, one of my favorite places to be is by the water. Are you serious, right now?"*

I said, "Yes, I would love that!"

He advised me not to get my hopes up, but stated he would reach out. "I know you need a placement where the church can afford to cover the cost of your internship stipend. There is an old Reformed Church on the island that can afford to do so. Jeff, the pastor there, has hosted many students. I think it will be a good fit for the church and you."

As soon as he mentioned the possibility, I knew that God would allow me to go. I had an incredible experience meeting an eclectic group of folks, all ages and backgrounds.

When I arrived on the island, despite the airline misplacing my luggage, and my being without a swimsuit for the church picnic at Magens Bay that day, I felt like I was at home. The old architecture and slow pace of the island culture resonated with me.

I preached, attended the consistory leadership meetings with the elders, led a study on the Psalms at Magens Bay, assisted My Brother's Workshop utilizing my Job Corps experience, and more.

I was privileged to be invited to visit a church member's elderly mother, who was quite ill. I instantly became very fond of them. I thought that was why the visits were so significant. That was only partially true. I would learn the following year when I did an extra internship that it was part of my calling and gifting.

Ministering to those who were sick and/or dying was surprisingly a sweet spot for me. God's Spirit moved in special ways to bless His people through the words I was led to share and the quiet, comforting moments. I found it to be such an honor and privilege to be present in those spaces with people.

My brother, Bruce, came down for a week. He picked out gold wedding bands to propose to Cheryl, his son's mother, again. They had been divorced for many years and were now back together again. I was able to join their pastor overseeing their marriage ceremony which I still cherish, especially since Cheryl has since passed.

I spent a lot of time at the beach. Magens Bay is gorgeous with a mile of beach perfect for walking. I tried to walk weekly with Shirley. Walking in the water helped to strengthen her core and her back began to straighten up.

The bay was where ideas would come together for my sermons. It was my favorite place to sit and have a talk with God. It was also where we ended up wrestling towards the end of my time there. Guess who won that match?

I have shared that I'm a "pretty smart cookie," perceptive and intuitive. I can also be obtuse at times, oblivious to what's right in front of me, slow on the uptake.

I had enrolled at seminary knowing that I had been led there by God. I thought it was to deepen my theological understanding and perhaps acquire more discipline. It never occurred to me that I would become part of the Reformed Church in America (RCA), which is the denomination the seminary is affiliated with. It is why I attempted to maintain my home church as my required "teaching church" during my first year.

Today, as I am enjoying the water and sunshine, the Lord begins telling me that I will be joining the RCA when we return to school in September.

I recoiled at the very thought of it. I was grateful for my first year, but I had experienced a significant amount of racism and sexism. Also, most of the folks I encountered seemed to either not know about the gifts of the Spirit or not to believe in them.

In case those two factors weren't enough reason not to join, I reminded God, *"These are the same people who owned and operated the slave castles we visited in Ghana. You know, the ones proclaiming to worship You while just below they were holding people as property in conditions worse than what folks might do to their animals."*

God assured me that He was aware of all this. I asked Him, *"Does this mean I will be serving in one of their churches when I graduate?"* Duh!

I will say He was very patient with me, holding me in a light grip as we wrestled, rather than body slamming me.

He replied, *"Yes."*

I said, *"I don't want to."* He already knew that and had His mind made up. Once I realized that I couldn't persuade Him to change His mind, I asked could I please not be assigned to a church in Grand Rapids, as it would feel too awkward. Also, might I go to one of their churches that had at least two or three people of color, and where His Spirit was clearly present.

He granted my request.

I had participated in a small group discussion after school hours that winter semester. One of the women had mentioned an RCA church in Muskegon where God's Spirit was moving. I believed that she had mentioned they also had a bit of diversity.

I couldn't remember the name of it to save my life. I asked the Holy Spirit to bring it back to my remembrance.

Matt had already informed me that I needed to find a church for the coming year to serve as my teaching church assignment. My current placement was not sufficient to complete my curriculum requirements. He had begun looking and had sent me to meet the pastor at Hope Reformed Church in Grand Rapids that spring prior to my leaving for St. Thomas.

I liked the pastor, but at that time they were looking for someone to work with youth. Although I had many years of experience, it wasn't what I felt led to do at that time.

After my conversation with the Lord on the beach, I reached out to Matt and informed him that I was coming into the denomination. "There's a church in Muskegon I'm interested in checking out as a possibility for my teaching church assignment these last two years. Someone mentioned them to me this spring, but I don't remember the name."

"Probably Fellowship Reformed," he says. He scheduled an interview with their pastor, Greg. When I walked into Greg's office, I saw pictures from Africa all over his walls. I said, "I want to go." He replied, "You will." He began telling me about their mission work in Uganda.

We hit it off right away. It was the perfect place for me to be as I accepted and adjusted coming into the denomination. God's Spirit was present, as were a few people of color. I was well-received by folks. There was one old man who informed me he didn't believe in women pastors. "You're ok, though. I like your spirit and preaching."

The women asked me to be the "guest speaker" for their women's day weekend. I was thrilled and honored. I couldn't believe that they were also paying me a speaker's fee! This was my first time presenting to a large group outside of preaching on a Sunday.

It was particularly special because of how this Muskegon congregation embraced and accepted me, as well as having my sister-in-law, Cheryl and my grandchildren's mom, Shika, present that Saturday.

I was filled with so much love and gratitude as I looked around the circle prior to sharing an Agape Feast to close out our time together.

The feast can be carried out in various forms. The simple communal meal and service is intended to promote fellowship, unity, and Christian love. The women were invited to share a red grape and a fish shaped cracker with someone. The grape and cracker symbolized the bread & wine served for traditional communion in the church. It was a reminder that we are all one in Christ. As they presented their offering to one another, each woman also spoke a word of gratitude and appreciation over their recipient to bless them.

I shared a small portion of this story at the conference. It was titled, "Climbing High to Reach Low." A couple of women put together mountain scenery and designed our invitations to the event.

I spoke about my struggles and overcoming by the grace of God. I shared that our ascent with God is an invitation to reach out to others who are still trapped in the struggle. I reaffirmed that we must share our experiences and knowledge so that others realize God will move on their behalf.

One of the women created an amazing labyrinth to complement the message. Music played softly. One stood at the entrance looking at oneself in a blurred glass. Upon entering, you were invited while walking through to pick up stones labeled with various negative thoughts, feelings, and behaviors. You selected whichever ones resonated with you. There were various signposts along the way. A Cross stood in the middle of the labyrinth. You left those stones, that negativity and pain, at the foot of the Cross. You continued your journey gathering stones with positive affirmations. You departed the labyrinth gazing at your true self in a clear mirror and emerged holding the fruit of the Spirit and God's promises to you.

I was invited to share the presentation at two other conferences, one in Grand Haven and the other in Grand Rapids.

A Word and a Sign

"A word fitly spoken is like apples of gold in settings of silver." – Proverbs 15:23 ESV

I became aware of the African American Black Caucus arm of the RCA towards the end of my second year in seminary. I was invited to attend their gathering in Philadelphia one weekend. The seminary covered the expenses.

It was so refreshing and invigorating to be surrounded by

people of color within the denomination. I found out that this was much more prominent on the East coast and in California.

I was even invited, as a newbie, to speak to the group at one of the sessions. This was intimidating for me in the presence of such scholars and great preachers, yet also a blessing.

Two unusual things happened during mornings in the breakfast area of the hotel. First, the staff went out of their way to be warm and welcoming, gracious, and helpful. I was being treated as if I was a celebrity. It was so over-the-top that I finally asked one of the workers about it.

He smiled and said, "You don't know?" To which I replied, "Know what?" He proceeded to tell me that I glow. He said, "The light that you carry is significant. It is very strong and bright. Most of us working in the dining room and kitchen are Believers. We all can see it."

I didn't understand, but I thanked him for telling me and for the wonderful service I was receiving. I held the words in my heart and pondered them.

I remembered being in a shop down in St. Thomas and a gentleman being drawn to me. I knew instinctively that it wasn't a natural attraction, but that he saw Christ in me. I thanked God for this gift and for letting me know that it happens sometimes. Although I can't see the light, being told that it is there, helps keep me aware of trying to make sure that I don't dim it. I marvel at God's grace.

One morning, at the conference, the breakfast nook was full. As I stood there scanning the room for an open seat with folks I knew, a gentleman invited me to share his table. I thanked him and sat down.

Pastor Alex was from Ghana. I told him that I had been privileged to visit his country. I spoke of my love for traveling. He told me that I would visit his continent many times. I mentioned the upcoming mission trip to Uganda, as well as my lack of funds.

He said, "You will go, Dear. Others will provide financial

support for your travels. You will stay in the homes of pastors or ministers. You will go several times. You will be like an African spiritual mother."

I thought about him when serving at the first church after seminary. Pastor Peter had taken a sabbatical during my last year. He brought back a gift for me, a beautiful painting on wood of a Black woman garbed in orange with a headdress, holding a baby. When I saw it my first thought was of Pastor Alex and his declaration of my becoming an "African mother."

I mentioned Pastor Alex's words to someone during my first trip to Egypt. He responded, "One has to spend much time here before being accepted and seen in that way." Later, after seeing me with the people, he noted with surprise, how quickly they were accepting me. I said, "Yes. I am one of them. This is my homeland. It is also one of the gifts that God does with me."

Returning from the caucus in Philadelphia, I would soon recall Alex's words as things begin to unfold at Fellowship.

Pastor Greg had moved on to another church during my last year in seminary. Kevin approached me to let me know we would soon be gearing up for the mission trip to Uganda. I said that there was no way I could afford to do that. He replied, "You're going. You will assist Jim visiting the folks who received micro-loans for their businesses." I did that and so much more!

Yvonne, who I affectionately called "Butterball," heard about the mission trip. "Deborah, you must send an email to your family members, friends, and associates. They will sponsor your trip to Uganda."

I responded that I couldn't do that. I had never heard of such a thing. "Oh, you must. You must raise the funds for the trip. They will send you." I was flabbergasted! "Really?" She said, "Yes, of course. People do this all the time." I responded, "You White folks really are amazing. I don't think we do this in the Black church."

She was right. Not only did folks sponsor me to go to Uganda, but later they would sponsor my ministry trips to Oman, Egypt (4x's), Jordan, Israel, and Palestine.

I stayed in the homes of bishops and pastors, or the church denomination's apartments where the ministers lived, just as Pastor Alex had prophesied. I would also travel to religious conferences, seminars, and retreats in Montreal, Pasadena, and Malibu at no expense to me.

God is truly amazing! As was the trip to Uganda. We all helped Kevin and the other dentist set up the clinic with all their supplies. I was assigned with Jim to visit some of the people who had received micro-loans. It was a group effort. Others would help the ones who had received a loan to be successful. Their ability to borrow hinged upon the current debtors paying their loans back on time. They all kept one another accountable.

We went out to the fields to see the women's crops. They shared how they planted with basic tools, no real equipment like one might see back in the States. Everyone would come out to assist at harvest time, both picking the crop, and helping get it to the local market.

There were many other business ventures as well. One of the nice things about checking out those enrolled in the program was the opportunity we had to visit many of their homes. We were able to see firsthand how they lived, meet others in the village, and hear their stories.

Bishop Stephen arranged for me to speak to over 1,500 students at three different schools. I shared the story of Joseph—how he was destined to serve his people, the hardships he endured, God's faithfulness even during adversity, and how he became second in command to Pharaoh in Egypt which allowed him to save his people during the Great Famine.

Jim noted how my storytelling improved each time. I smiled. Practice does make perfect. I was standing talking to a couple of people afterwards at the last school. One of the students was waiting patiently to speak to me. I turned and said, "Hello." He was beaming as he straightened his shoulders, while responding, "I am Joseph." He was letting me know that he had heard and received the message. He was committed to living not only for himself and his family, but also for his community and his country. My heart was full. My cup over-flowed. I praised and thanked God for this privilege.

Bishop then told me I would be speaking at a service for retired pastors and widows. I balked! I let him know that there was no way I could speak to these men who had spent their lives preaching. I didn't have anything to share given their years of experience. He replied, "Perhaps you don't, but the Holy Spirit does. He will speak through you."

I sought God and began to prepare the message. Relief washed over me during the service as the Call to Worship, songs, and Scripture text that had been chosen all aligned with the Word I would be preaching.

I greeted the widows. "I am so honored to be invited to share with you today. I have no idea how you must feel or what your lives are like since losing your husbands. I can only imagine. However, I watched my mother survive as a widow these past 25 years. I witnessed her sorrow and her joys. I watched as she carved out a meaningful life without her partner. So, I do feel connected to you, your sorrow, and hardship." Personalizing the message with my mother's experience caused them to shift their posture and open themselves up to me. I could tell that I was being accepted.

I then spoke to the retired pastors, "Thank you for your life of service. I must again acknowledge that I don't have the experience or wisdom to speak to you either—yet, I will trust the Holy Spirit to use me as an empty vessel. I trust that He will pour into me so that I may pour out and serve all of you."

They thanked me and were attentive. God, of course, was faithful and spoke an on-time Word to everyone.

"We are grateful for your service and sacrifice. But I must

remind you that although you are retired and there has been a significant shift, the work is not yet done until you see God face to face. There is a new invitation for you to mentor and coach the young men and women. There is a sacred place for sharing all your wisdom and gifts with the communities you love."

At the end of the service, I received an unimaginable gift. Bishop asked them to share what they heard from God through my message. I was blown away! God is so generous and kind.

Later, after graduating and joining Hope Church as their Community Engagement Pastor, I shared tales of my adventure in Uganda with the congregation. I mentioned the need for clean water.

One of the men stopped by my office one day to talk about Uganda. Ted informed me that he and his wife had given money many years before, when their child was a student at Hope College, towards a mission trip sponsoring clean water.

The trip didn't happen. The money had just been sitting in the account at the college ever since. Ted said, "Nancy and I are going to request the school return the funds to us. It can then be used for clean water in Uganda."

We arranged for the money to be forwarded to Bishop Stephen. Three wells were built in proximity to schools. The schools are at the heart of communities. Placing the wells there provided both for the students as well as the families in the immediate area.

I see the marvelous web that God forms over and over, various ripple effects, relationships between people that connect dots creating scenarios—even so I am always amazed. I am increasingly aware of our connectedness and the importance of being faithful, especially in the little things that we tend to think don't matter. God uses everything.

Providence & Breadcrumbs

"Walk in obedience to all that the Lord your God has commanded you, so that you may live and prosper and prolong your days in the land that you will possess." – Deuteronomy 5:3 NIV

Early during the last year of seminary, students were beginning to search for possible church assignments. They would send out their curriculum vitae (CV) in hopes of securing interviews and offers.

Mid-year some of the students began asking me which churches out East I was considering. I responded that as much as I would like to move out East, I was staying here in Michigan. They were surprised and clumsily searched for their next words. What they were struggling not to say is that there would be few opportunities for an older, Black woman in the Midwest.

I helped them out by sharing that I wasn't searching anywhere for a placement. I told them, "God has not brought me to seminary at this stage of my life to leave me searching. His plan for me includes my placement after seminary." They said, "Yes, but you have to follow the process." To which I would reply, "You're right. But I am to follow His process for me, not the system's."

I appreciated their confusion. I don't know many people who walk with God in the bizarre way that I do. Nor have I met many people who cried out to Him the way I did asking for Him to order their steps. He threw me a lifeline that I continue to hold on to.

At the end of the first year, prior to going down to St. Thomas, Matt sent me to Hope Reformed Church in Grand Rapids to meet the pastor. As I noted previously, I wasn't led to become involved with youth work.

My second year of seminary I was at a Redbox outside a CVS store. A guy across the parking lot yelled out to me. "Hey, how are you? Do you remember me? How's seminary going?" It was

Pastor Peter from Hope Church. We chatted for a moment. I was impressed that he remembered me.

My last year of seminary I believed that God was indicating that I would be going to serve at Hope Church. Therefore, I was taken by surprise and caught off guard when I heard the Holy Spirit tell me to apply for a position with the denomination's African American Black Caucus.

I was confused. I shared this with God, telling Him that I didn't understand. I reminded Him of our wrestling for me to come into the denomination. I shared examples of how He had changed and prepared my heart to be a pastor. How He had slowly, patiently changed my opinion and beliefs around women even becoming pastors.

"Now that I want to be a pastor you are telling me to do some-thing else?" I resisted. His instruction to apply remained firm. The deadline was fast approaching. Finally, just prior to leaving for the mission trip to Uganda, I sent off my CV to the RCA.

Weeks went by and I had not heard anything. I let the Lord know that I was now really confused. I was certain He had told me to apply for the position. I knew that I wasn't the strongest candidate for the job, but since God had told me to apply, I thought something was going to happen.

Something did. The Director of Human Resources finally called to interview me. We had an amazing conversation that lasted over an hour. I later learned that the church she was a member of had been talking about becoming more multicultural. They were going to hire a person of color, as their Pastor of Community Engagement.

She told the pastor about "this woman" she had just inter-viewed who she believed would be a perfect fit for the position they were creating.

At one point, she mentioned my name. He said, "I know her. I've met her." Pastor Peter emailed me and asked if I was open to having a conversation. We met and discussed the church's desire to become more multicultural and the new Assistant Pastor position they were creating. I had conversations with various members of the leadership team. And, I was invited to preach.

My spirit was correct in discerning that God was going to place me at Hope Reformed Church. The pathway there was not one that anyone could have known or planned. It depended upon various intersections and connections, hearing God's leading, and my obedience. Had I not applied for the position with the denomination, Sharon would not have been aware of me and recommended me to Pastor Peter and the church for consideration.

There are times when what God is sharing, where and how He is leading me, doesn't make any sense in the natural realm. I confess, there are still moments when I question, or even tell Him that something isn't clear, it doesn't add up. That is true less and less though. The longer I walk with Him and see how He navigates my life, the easier it has become to just go with the flow. I generally trust and obey. Doing so has allowed me to meet the most wonderful people, given me access to interesting learning experiences and events, and allowed me to travel to the most amazing places.

It is not an easy way to live though. Many family members and friends don't understand. They think I am crazy. Some don't believe I hear the voice of God in the specific ways that I say. I get it. Also, by their standards I am not financially stable and secure. The wealth I have is not financial, but it is significant. Yet, most often I can't see around the corner what's coming up next. It generally is not revealed until the very last moment. I don't know how God is going to supply a need. I must trust that He is and that it will be on time.

HICCUPS ALONG THE WAY

LIGHT AFFLICTIONS

"For our light and momentary troubles are achieving for us an eternal glory that far outweighs them all." – 2 Corinthians 4:17 NIV

Is My Brother My Keeper?

"A friend loveth at all times; And a brother is born for adversity." – Proverbs 17:17 KJV

My eldest brother, Bruce drove the U-Haul truck when God relocated me to Holland for seminary. He was so proud of me! He could be your best friend or your harshest critic. This was due to both his personality and the demons he wrestled with. Mother often teased that despite our age differences, in many ways, he and I were twins.

Growing up, and I guess even into adulthood, he was very much my hero. I could depend on him most of the time. I understood and was clear those times when I couldn't—like when I was sitting in that jail cell.

I knew that he wanted the best for me. He didn't give up on me. So, it was extremely difficult my last year of seminary when things went sideways. I was so stressed between the issue of whether I would have to take Greek and Hebrew, and the disintegration of my relationship with him, that I had begun having panic attacks.

His wife, Cheryl, was ill. She told Bruce that she needed me. She wanted to be able to talk to me and see me. She said that he must reconcile, or at least make enough peace with me, so that she and I could resume our relationship. Things had disintegrated such that he didn't even come to my graduation. It was the progression of her illness that eventually brought us back together.

They are both with the Lord now. She passed in 2015. I miss her terribly. He transitioned two days after my birthday in 2022. Words don't begin to describe the void that exists with his absence.

Yes, Sometimes It Can Be Quite Bumpy

"I remain confident of this; I will see the goodness of the Lord in the land of the living. Wait for the Lord; be strong and take heart and wait for the Lord." – Psalm 27:13-14 NIV

I attended the RCA General Synod at Central College in Pella, Iowa as a non-voting, seminary delegate that spring the month after graduation.

I knew by this point that I was going to Hope Church even though nothing had been finalized yet.

There weren't many people of color at the Synod. This was not surprising. Many people were friendly and gracious, reaching out to introduce themselves to me and others who were new to the denomination.

One of the men inquired if we could have lunch one day. I consented. He was an attorney and considered himself to be a prominent member of his church. Unbeknownst to me, he was a member of Hope Church. He thought that I knew who he was since I had preached there. I did not.

He proceeded to share the long history of the church, including his disappointment that they had missed an opportunity to sell the building to Walgreen's when they were looking for a new site on Kalamazoo Ave. He mentioned the church leadership's prior conversations with two male Black pastors about joining the ministry team. In his opinion they were not a good fit, as both had too many new ideas and wanted too much autonomy. He was presently of the mindset that the church should just close and give the remaining funds to the denomination.

He then informed me that the church would never offer me a Call to Minister. I held it together while attempting to eat my lunch and remain attentive.

Once he finished his discourse, I politely thanked him, walked quickly to the nearest women's bathroom, and began to sob. Just then Pastor Peter's sister walked into the bathroom, embraced me with a hug, and asked what was wrong.

I shared my lunch experience with her. She called her brother who was on vacation. He phoned me and apologized. He said the man was totally out of order. He was not a current leader in the church. He was stating his own opinion. He hoped that the incident would not deter me from coming there to serve. I assured him that it wouldn't since it was God's choice, not mine.

Ken was right. The church did not offer me a Call. I was also correct. God did place me there. I received an initial 2-year contract with full benefits, which was extended for an additional year.

An Unexpected Bill

"Do not be anxious about anything, but in everything by prayer and supplication with thanksgiving let your requests be made known to God." – Philippians 4:6 ESV

I was receiving unemployment funds my first year in school. I left for my internship in St. Thomas shortly after classes wrapped up. Pastor Jeff told me not to forward my mail as I would be back in the States before it would reach me. I had arranged for one of my neighbors to bring in the mail and water my plants.

While I was gone a notice came from the unemployment bureau requesting an update on my school status. It had an early August deadline which I missed.

Upon my return, as I went through all the mail, I found the letter from the unemployment office. I immediately responded, sending them my grades, confirmation of my internship, and an explanation of why I had missed their deadline.

They did not acknowledge consideration of my factors. Their position was that I had received the funds in error. I now owed the money back along with interest and penalties.

God told me not to send a single dollar or it would be an acknowledgement that I was responsible. Instead, I sent another letter. I sent letters the last two years of seminary and my first year serving at the church following graduation. No one ever seemed to look at the matter and consider the unreasonableness of their position.

My second year at the church, as I was preparing to send my bi-annual response, the Holy Spirit said, *"Send everything that you sent the very first time."* This would have included my grades for that semester, proof of my internship, when it started, the fact that my mail had not been forwarded, and the date I returned from the island.

I told the Holy Spirit, as if He didn't already know; *"They already have all that information."* He repeated that I was to send everything that I had sent the first time. I was obedient.

I made copies, sealed the envelope, and anointed it with oil. I took it to Pastor Peter. "You probably don't understand this or agree with this request, but you're my spiritual covering. I need you to lay hands on this envelope and pray for a positive resolution." Out of respect for me, he did so. I mailed it, praying that the person who handled it would read it and have basic common sense.

One day I received a letter stating that they had reviewed my case and I didn't owe anything. It was written in legal jargon stating the position in reverse. I decided to call and confirm my understanding.

The original bill was for just over $12,000. It had now ballooned with over $48,000 in interest and penalties. The total amount owed on the last statement I received was more than $65,000. I still have that statement as a reminder of what God can and will do, if we just hang on and trust His Word.

I prayed that the person who answered my call would be patient and thorough. She was. I told her why I was calling, that I wanted to confirm my understanding of what the letter I had just received said. After reading it to her, she replied, "Yes, I believe you are correct."

"May I place you on hold while I confirm with my supervisor?" "Yes, absolutely! Take all the time you need." After waiting a bit, she came back on line apologizing for the delay, "You have a very thick file." "Yes, I know. I've been writing for the past few years."

"Your understanding is correct. The decision has been reversed upon receiving new information." I told her that I hadn't sent anything new. "What piece of information has turned things around?" She replied, "They received your grades and information about your internship." I told her that I had sent my grades and internship information the first time I addressed the matter. I thought to myself about the Holy Spirit telling me to send everything I had sent the first time. I thanked God.

I then proceeded to tell her that the previous year the State of Michigan had withheld my income tax refund because this debt was showing on the books. I asked who I needed to contact to now receive my refund. She was surprised that I was asking for it. I explained that since it was taken in error it should now be returned to me. She conceded advising she would put a request in the system. I thanked her and asked for a name and number of someone in that area to follow up with.

I received that check just in time for my next trip to provide pulpit supply in St. Thomas.

Approximately four years after receiving the bill in error, the matter was finally addressed in my favor, eliminating a $65,000 debt that I shouldn't have been charged, and the return of my income tax refund!

This outcome would not have been possible if I had not heard and been obedient when God said not to send even a dollar towards the debt. Or, if I had disregarded the Holy Spirit leading me to resend all my original proof of dispute documents.

Can you imagine how this encourages me even today to seek God's voice and walk in obedience? Remembering what I consider to be some of God's miracles in my life causes my faith to soar whenever I reflect on it.

Fine Tuning

"Therefore, brethren, be even more diligent to make your call and election sure, for if you do these things you will never stumble;" – 2 Peter 1:10 NKJV

Now that I had joined the denomination, I felt led to offer myself for a second internship so that I could more fully immerse myself in the culture.

Matt thought this was an excellent idea and offered to look for a church that would cover my 10-week stipend that second summer. He located a church in New Jersey.

The pastor and the consistory vice-president called to interview me. I hit it off immediately with the pastor. The VP mentioned, "We are a rather wealthy congregation in a small, well-to-do town." I didn't respond. She mentioned it again and I thought, *"I'm not opposed to wealth.*" She noted it a few more times throughout our conversation. I was slow, but my "Aha" moment finally arrived. I smiled, as I recognized what she was really saying. She knows that I am Black and doesn't think I will fit in.

I called one of my professors, whom I had never previously sought out for advice. I told him what had happened. He just so happened to know the pastor. He reached out to him and confirmed my suspicion was correct. "He really wants you to come out there. And, you will be fine."

"How can you proclaim that with such confidence given how that woman showed me her true colors, which are probably a reflection of most of the folks in that town?"

"I believe that God is making the selection, and who you are, your background, everything has prepared you to both fit in and to handle the assignment." He then provided an example, comparing me to another Black student and sharing how although it was wrong, I could fit in where she would not be able to, based upon our upbringings.

The irony is that she was much more "Reformed" than I am. Her knowledge and familiarity with the theology and doctrinal language are much stronger than mine.

What he was referring to was my growing up middle-class and the fact that she didn't. He noted how my time in the Episcopal Church, at the University of Michigan, Aquinas College, and other factors would be assets for me. As much as I didn't like it, I knew that he was right.

I informed Matt of my interview. I told him that I was going to accept the assignment. I asked him not to say anything to the pastor. I was merely sharing the incident as an example of what the students of color sometimes encounter and endure being in the denomination.

In addition to the parsonage, the church owned an additional home two doors over. This is where I was to reside for the summer. It was furnished with a lumpy bed that caused my sciatic nerve to flare up, one uncomfortable chair, and one or two straight chairs. I generally sat on the floor with pillows. I had one straight chair that I could sit in while I ate my meals on a T.V. tray. I often wondered if I had been White whether they would have put some decent furniture in the house.

They held a traditional service in the old, original church building. The building that housed the offices and preschool also had a large sanctuary for contemporary worship on Sundays.

My first time preaching in the old church I saw an older man peeking through the doorway. Upon seeing that I would be preaching, he turned around and left. I'm not sure if it was because I am female, Black, or both. I don't know if he went to the contemporary service or back home. I didn't particularly care.

My first couple of weeks I would count the number of Black folks I saw as I moved around town. I mentioned it to one of the clerks at the grocery store. She laughed. "We don't live here in town. Anyone you encounter working in a business resides somewhere else." My count was at about nine people at that point. I had to drop it down to just one, besides myself. I'm sure there were probably a few more.

I knew that there was a Black woman who was a member of the church, but I never saw her. She never attended services, nor did she make any effort to welcome a fellow "sister." I found this to be peculiar. Clearly, she didn't consider me to be one, nor feel compelled to offer any hospitality.

The second weekend following my arrival, the youth held a car wash in the parking lot. There was an older gentleman there. He spoke with me for a bit. Then he assured me, "You're going to be ok."

"You just met me. How do you know that?"

He just smiled. "Trust me," he said. "You will be fine."

Evenings, weekends, and Sundays after church, I was alone. It wasn't until I had been there a few weeks, and made a comment to someone in the office, that anyone asked me out to do anything. Once we had that conversation, I did begin forming relationships with a few folks.

I had a girlfriend who lived on Long Island in New York. She told me to start coming up for their afternoon church service. Soon after, she told me to come for the Wednesday evening Bible studies. She offered to pay my toll fees and treated me to dinner on Sundays.

God gave me a lifeline through her. The other gifts He gave me were a hospital visit soon after arriving and house calls. The family at the hospital couldn't believe that I came up to see their loved one, given that I was an intern who had just arrived that week. They were so grateful.

Although I had one guy who wouldn't answer his door for a visit, others were glad to see me. They, too, were most appreciative. I surprisingly discovered what a privilege it is to be invited into those moments of illness and/or pending death.

After preaching God's Word, I treasure those opportunities and privileges most in my time as a pastor. It is one of my sweet spots in ministry, being invited into those spaces. Often when I enter a sacred space, it is as if I slip into the background. The Holy Spirit is front and center, ministering to His people. There are times when I am praying or comforting someone, when He is speaking and moving through me in such a way that I am not really participating. I couldn't tell you afterwards what was said because I didn't say it. He did. It is why those moments, those spaces, are so sacred. The Holy Spirit engulfs us. I experienced this many times when doing ministry outside of the country.

A Lesson in the Blessing

"Consider it all joy, my brethren, when you encounter various trials." – James 1:2 NASB

I was invited back to St. Thomas Reformed Church the next three summers. I provided pulpit supply while Jeff was on vacation.

My first time on the island during my 10-week internship, I stayed at an amazing house on a cliff overlooking the ocean. I was there two weeks while the Bible camp folks took over my spot in the parsonage. Another time I was invited back to house sit for this couple. There was a breathtaking view, a short walk down to the beach, and a pool to float in at night while stargazing and watching the asteroids.

That year God told me to invite a woman that I met during my internship at the RCA Church in New Jersey. Her mother had recently passed and she needed a respite. The homeowners allowed her to stay in the adjoining cottage.

My last summer on the island, Mikki, my best friend, traveled down with me. We both stayed in the parsonage. It would be one of our last trips together.

She was there the Saturday that my wallet with my driver's license, bank card, cash, and the flash drive with the next day's sermon on it were stolen. I had left the car keys under a towel on a picnic table while I walked the beach, which was customary; all the locals did the same.

I was at my favorite place to hangout talking with God, as previously noted. I would walk the beach or just sit looking out at the horizon while tightening up a sermon in my mind.

As I walked back approaching the picnic table, I noticed a guy sitting at a table close by. My radar went off. I immediately knew something was wrong. He proceeded to ask me, "Is that old, blue car over there yours?"

"Why?" I ask.

"I saw someone rummaging around inside the car," he said.

I ran up to the picnic table. The car key was not under my towel. The car door is locked. I know that he has the car key. I was sure that all of my items were gone, including the keys for the church, offices, and the parsonage.

"How did you know that I was driving that car? It belongs to the church. I'm preaching there tomorrow. The flash drive with my sermon on it is in there. I don't live here. I need my license to fly home." I really began to panic!

He pretended like he was helping me look for the thief. "You know," he said, "We should report this to the park manager." As we headed in that direction, he said, "Let me just check the bathroom." He never returned.

By this time, I was beginning to panic. I was crying as I walked towards the front of the park to find the manager. One of the ladies from church saw me and ran over to find out what was happening. I told her.

We went back over to the car. My phone was now on the front seat. I said, "He's been back in the car. He must have taken the car keys and then saw me walking up the beach approaching him. He waited until after I was gone to find the park manager to get in the car and steal everything."

"My wallet with my driver's license is gone so I won't be able to board the plane to return home." She responded, "We will intervene so that they can expedite a new one, or papers from the government to allow you to fly home."

I blubbered through my tears, "Tomorrow's sermon is on my stolen flash drive." She calmly told me, "The message is already written on your heart. God will deliver it tomorrow if you show up."

I mentioned that not only the car keys, but all the church keys were gone. "There are spare keys at the parsonage," she said. "I'll go get the keys and tell Mikki what is going on." I later learned that she and Mikki prayed for a positive outcome, "Nothing missing, nothing broken."

As I walked back towards the front of the park to locate the manager, I thought, *"I hope you drop dead for doing this."* I realized that what I was thinking was wrong, that I should cast down that thought immediately. Instead, I spoke it aloud. I could try to use my distraught emotions in that moment as an excuse, but despite my panicked state, I knew better. I immediately asked God to forgive me because I knew it was wrong.

The park manager approached me, so I told him what had happened and described the young man. He said, "Oh, I know him. He's a good kid. He didn't do it." I said, "No, you're wrong. He's the thief." He didn't believe it.

We walked back to the car. I explained all the details on the way. I looked in the car, told him that the phone was now gone from the front seat, so he had once again been in the car while I was gone.

While I was peering into the car, the manager glanced around the car. He noticed a trail in the sand going underneath the SUV parked next to the car. I got down on my knees to look. There were the car keys! The thief had thrown them under the vehicle and left.

I retrieved the keys, unlocked the car, and opened the glove compartment. The church keys, my phone, flash drive, and wallet were all intact. My license, debit card, cash, and everything was still in the small clutch! Nothing was missing, nothing was broken!

I thanked God and once again asked Him to forgive me. I prayed that He used this event to soften the young man's heart and bring him into the Kingdom.

I am very careful now, not only about my thoughts, but certainly the words that I speak to myself and others.

The next morning, at the end of the service, I shared this event with the congregation. I needed to confess my brokenness to the body of Christ, along with God's grace and forgiveness. Several of the ladies' stated that someone had been stealing from them all summer as they exercised on the beach. We prayed that it had come to an end. We believed in Christ for the young man's salvation.

A few years later, after the event with the unemployment bureau came to a positive resolution, God told me that He holds time, and He holds me. It may happen suddenly like on the beach, or it may take years like with the unemployment debt—but He is always in control. He has me. I remind myself of this, as needed.

Speaking in Other Languages, But Not Tongues

"But Moses said before the Lord, "Behold, I am unskilled in speech; how then will Pharoah listen to me?" – Exodus 6:30 NASB

The Master of Divinity degree had a language requirement. One had to pass both Greek and Hebrew courses. I knew that I couldn't learn those languages. I had enrolled with an intention to learn theology. It didn't matter to me whether I obtained a degree; I desired learning.

God changed all of that on the beach at Magens Bay with His declaration that I join the denomination. I was now floundering, totally lost in my Greek class. I spoke to my advisor. I was told that a waiver may be extended to those students who have a learning disability. I didn't have a disability, but I inquired about that process. It was expensive, even with the seminary paying a portion.

I was scheduled for an evaluation. The man conducting the interview and testing was very insecure, and most likely racist and misogynistic. Even so, I must meet with him twice.

During our first interaction, he was amazed at how quickly and accurately I could complete the assessment. I reminded him that my deficiency was with languages, not numbers, sequencing, or memory. He didn't appreciate the information, or agree with the distinction. He responded, "That may be, but if you can do these tests so readily, you can learn Greek or Hebrew." I realized that he was neither smart, logical, nor compassionate. I was in trouble.

At our next session, he proceeded to psychoanalyze, me sharing his perceived beliefs about my emotional baggage and hangups. He conveyed that I clearly had a problem with authority figures.

He informed the school that I didn't have a learning disability. That was, in fact, true. I knew that when I scheduled to try and fail the assessment. Unfortunately, I was not able to.

I wondered what was going to happen. God assured me that it wouldn't be an issue; I would not have to take the languages. My cousin, Janice, prayed about it. She informed me that God had confirmed this with her, as well.

I had dropped Greek that semester. I signed up for Hebrew one semester, but withdrew. I applied to take Greek online through an approved school. My thinking was that if I could do it at my own pace, I could prepare myself to take the second year of Greek. This plan failed.

I did enroll in the 2nd year class, but I rarely attended after the instructor embarrassed me in front of the entire class. I didn't know how to do the work, so I stopped going. I went to Uganda for 10 days instead.

I was double-minded. I knew that God had said I would not have to take the languages and I would complete my degree, but I couldn't see how. I moved forward ordering my pictures, cap & gown, and preparing for graduation. I also applied for financial aid and housing for another year. I thought perhaps I might have to spend an additional year just learning the languages with no other classes.

The registrar let administration know that I was planning on staying another year. A meeting was convened with all the professors. They agreed to an alternative course of action that would allow them to waive the language requirements for me. This was the plan that was offered to students who did have a bona-fide learning disability. I had a huge extra, in-depth, written assignment to complete. I ended up taking an oral exam the morning of my graduation. Can you imagine the stress of it all?

God was true to his Word. I did not take Greek or Hebrew. I graduated with honors and completed my RCA exams with the Muskegon Classis that Spring.

THE LAST CHAPTER, TRANSITIONING

CELEBRATING ACCOMPLISHMENT

*"The Lord has done great things for us; we
are glad." – Psalm 126:3 ESV*

God's grace was sufficient! I made it! What He ordained for me began to unfold. Family and friends came to celebrate my graduation with me.

We rejoiced, not only at what I had achieved, but even more so we marveled at God: His faithfulness, His provision, His constancy even amid the turmoil, even with my big brother's absence. I held onto His never-changing hand and He brought me through!

My ordination service at Fellowship Reformed Church in Muskegon was glorious – just perfect! God's presence was so sweet. I was surrounded by people who loved, supported, and believed in me.

My professor, Rev. Dr. Carol Bechtel, who had marked up my paper with red ink at the beginning of my journey, proclaimed in my last class that she now had to give me an A on all my papers—my writing had improved that much, partially due to the fact that my work demanded it.

She honored me by agreeing to preach at my ordination service.

The woman whom I continuously grow in love and affection towards, who has walked with me since those beginning times in seminary, my spiritual director, Rev. Celaine Bouma-Prediger, gave the Charge to the Minister.

Fellowship Church hosted a wonderful reception after the service. It was such a joy watching the diverse group of my biological family and friends, my Fellowship family, colleagues, and new seminary friends mingle with one another. They are an amazing gift that I am eternally grateful for.

In Between

"Let the favor of the Lord our God be upon us, and establish the work of our hands upon us; yes, establish the work of our hand!" – Psalm 90:17 ESV

Earlier, towards the end of my last year, God had introduced me to a gentleman who has a heart for the denomination and churches being more diverse.

Dave made it a point to provide introductions for me. I assured him that God had me covered. He was already preparing the place where I would be going. But I really appreciated his heart and sincerity.

I ended up serving on the Great Lakes Urban Ministry board for a season with him which allowed me to meet some exceptional people and gain much insight.

Dave was shorthanded for an upcoming youth group he was overseeing in Benton Harbor. He reached out to me wondering if I would be willing to help. He suggested that it was an opportunity for me to make a few extra dollars while waiting to start at the church in Grand Rapids. A win – win for both of us.

I immediately fell in love with Benton Harbor. I knew a bit of their history, of being this Black town that struggled for decades while their next door, White neighbor, St. Joseph was wealthy and thriving.

Dave introduced me to ministers and folks in the area. I attended a neighborhood Bible study. I joined him and the youth group at some of their work sites.

One Wednesday evening, the youth assisted at First Presbyterian Church serving the evening meal to folks from the community. They hung out, talking with people and engaging the smaller children in arts and crafts.

On the weekend, a street preacher set up on the corner right across the way from where we were staying. It was a hoot sitting outside listening to him and watching the kids' reactions.

This was the first time many of them had been around people of color. The excursion afforded them a broad, varied stroke of the culture. It was right up my alley! Little did I know at the time that Benton Harbor and First Presbyterian Church were threads that would be woven into my future path.

Pastor

"The Lord will guide you always; he will satisfy your needs in a sun-scorched land and will strengthen your frame. You will be like a well-watered garden, like a spring whose waters never fail." – Isaiah 58:11 NIV

Mission accomplished! I completed seminary, was ordained, and joined Hope Reformed Church as their Pastor of Community Engagement for three years.

It was challenging, joyous, painful, fulfilling, disappointing, surprising, and rewarding all in one.

I am forever grateful for the people and the experience.

I served part-time at Grace Christian Reformed Church for a year. I was charged with reigniting their community engagement and rebooting their Family Life Initiative (FLI) programming.

We ran a FLI program while I was at Hope Church, so I welcomed this opportunity to continue with some of the families while recruiting new ones to participate.

I also commuted to Benton Harbor for three months the summer following my departure from Hope Church. Dave sent me the notice letting me know the pastor at First Presbyterian was taking a sabbatical. Another God connection! The church had a multicultural congregation. They were very open and welcoming towards me. It was a gift to serve without being under attack by members of the congregation.

At the end of that summer, I was approached by Eastminster Presbyterian Church to serve part-time as their Lead Co-Pastor, which I accepted. I served five- and one-half years, retired, and began working on this book. All of these steps were ordered by the Lord.

CHANGE

"Behold, I am doing a new thing; now it springs forth, do you not perceive it? I will make a way in the wilderness and rivers in the desert." – Isaiah 43:19 ESV

Looks Can Be Deceiving

"For the Lord sees not as man sees; for man looks at the outward appearance, but the Lord looks at the heart." – 1 Samuel 16:7 AMP

There will be many who, upon reading my story, are shocked and repulsed by the knowledge of me serving as a pastor and engaging in other forms of ministry given the extent of my personal struggles. That's all right. I get it. They probably haven't read the stories of normal, everyday, fallen people in the Bible. They overlook the murderers, adulterers, and prostitutes who became kings, leaders, evangelists, and members of our Lord's family tree.

I have always looked like that nice, middle-class young woman—well, older now. Like the women in the halfway house, many folks think I look like a teacher—whatever that means.

My point is that I in no way, form, or fashion look like what

I have been through. God's grace has always shielded and preserved me.

I have been divorced since December 1996. I have been single and celibate for decades now. Some might think this is a punishment for my younger days. We do reap what we sow, but God is not punishing me for that which has been forgiven and redeemed.

He knows my heart – that I desire a husband, a partner. He may, or may not, have one for me. If He does, His timing will be perfect. I don't imagine that I would have experienced seminary, or visited so many places, if I had been married at the time.

I will certainly need someone who can love all of me, my past, present, and future without judgment or embarrassment. If he does come along one of these days, he will be uniquely crafted by God for me, exceptional, and well-worth the wait.

I encourage you to remember that looks are deceiving; they don't tell the true story of who we are. Our past doesn't cancel out the future that God has ordained for us. God redeems our past.

God looks at our hearts. He accepts us just as we are. He picks us up, and not only cleans us off, but also saves and sanctifies us. "There is no condemnation to those who are in Christ Jesus," Romans 8:1. We truly are the righteousness of God in Christ.

Our past actions do not define who we are. We are more than the worst thing we may have done or that has happened to us. Our new identity is found in Christ. And, like the prodigal son, we are always welcome, at any point in our journey, to return home to our heavenly Father.

Embracing the Charge

"God, your God, will restore everything you lost; he'll have compassion on you; he'll come back and pick up the pieces from all the places where you were scattered…and bring you back to the land your ancestors once possessed. It will be yours again." – Deuteronomy 30:3,5a MSG

"For still the vision awaits its appointed time; it hastens to the end — it will not lie. If it seems slow, wait for it; it will surely come; it will not delay." — Habakkuk 2:3 ESV

I've been walking closely with the Lord these past 29 years. I still marvel at "the goodness of the Lord in the land of the living" (Psalm 27:13).

I switched over from Debbie to Deborah when I turned 30. Of course, my family still calls me Debbie -- some, even Deb, which I disdain.

Abba, God, my Father holds all of them, from the little girl, my dad's "Deb-Deb," to Deborah the mature woman.

Unfortunately, some have painted a picture of God being mean, harsh, and judgmental, ready to punish us rather than forgive us. It is so untrue!

Too many of us have no real image of a father because that person has been absent. Or, our fathers have not been loving, gentle, and affirming with us, but rather negligent and/or abusive in a variety of ways.

We are broken. God is not. He is love. He does not choose to love or not love. He *is* love. It is impossible for Him to not show you love.

The picture that I hold of Him is shared in the story of *The Prodigal Son.* The son has wasted his fortune; he is now hanging around with the wrong crowd, homeless, and wallowing with the pigs.

His father is longing for him and patiently waiting. He is constantly looking out the window in hopes of seeing his son coming up the walkway. When he does, he runs out to greet him, kissing him on his neck.

This is the true revelation of our God. This is our Abba, Father God, who is eagerly waiting for you.

He reminds me that He has always been there with me, patiently, lovingly waiting for me to fully turn to Him.

He invites you to do the same. It's hard to imagine that all of the pain and negativity in your life can fall away, but the miraculous reality is that it truly can.

God places you back on His potter's wheel, softens all those hard things, and re-forms them. They are still a part of you, but in such a way that they no longer harm you or haunt you. Rather, they become part of your strength and grace. They are ammunition in your arsenal of wisdom and blessings for others.

It seems too good to be true that you can begin again, that it's not too late; there is a fresh future awaiting you. It seems impossible that you can create and embrace a new life and new opportunities with Him. Yet, all of it is true. I promise. I live it every day. Truly our latter days may be greater than our former ones.

I continue to believe in all of the possibilities my future holds. I continue to move forward, embracing my "Charge to the Minister."

> *"But you are not just a teller of stories, you are also a **holder of stories**... God's gentle unfolding of love and mercy in your life has hollowed and hallowed you to be a vessel for others. To listen to their stories, to hold them and to offer those stories up to God for safe keeping. **SO, I charge you to be a vessel**—a holding place—to hold God's mercy and love for your brothers and sisters in pain. May you always listen to those stories, and hold them just as you hold your own story. You will both hold and offer God's hands and heart for others, God's love and mercy for those in pain, and you have been emptied out for this purpose."*

This book is part of that charge. By God's grace, I will continue to hold and tell my own story, while holding those of others.

I will continue to love and pray for all of you with broken wings, knowing that God is awaiting you to turn to Him for healing, so that you, too, may fly.

ACKNOWLEDGMENTS

I must confess that I don't consider myself a writer in the traditional sense. Writing a thesis for a class or a sermon for the congregation is remarkably different than drafting one's memoir; or at least for me that is the case.

Yet, I am certain that God spoke to me about sharing my story. Thus, this offering is my act of obedience. As I began the journey, I wasn't certain if it was merely a final stage of healing for me, or something for you as well. My prayer is that God will place it in the hands of those who need to know that He is a healer. My hope is that you will discover that shame, regrets, fear, and guilt can be banished by the Spirit of God. I pray that you discover that you are beautifully and wonderfully made. And, that you are not defined by your past – what has happened to you, or what you have done. All things become new in Him. I hope you realize that it is never too late. God redeems not only you, but time. He defines who you are. You can begin anew. His purpose for you is still here. You are invited to embrace new life. As with me, your latter years can also be greater than your former ones. God truly is amazing! He loves us so much!

I would like to thank my family, who have always loved and supported me – no matter what. Thank you to my son, David, who truly is beloved; and to all my wonderful grandchildren. After Jesus, come all of you! Thank you to my friends (past and present). Thank you to everyone that I have encountered on my journey – good and bad. God used you to refine me. Thank you to Ms. Barbara Gordon, who believed in me enough to provide support for the book to be published. Ann Saigon, SaraJane Herrboldt, and Rev. Mandy Fowler thanks for reading portions of my draft and offering feedback. I especially would like to thank my sister-in-the Spirit, Tamber, who has walked with me through this process praying and encouraging me. Thank you, Sis for the title – Reviving the Ruins. It truly resonates with me as I acknowledge – The Reconstruction of My Fractured Soul.

ABOUT THE AUTHOR

Reverend Deborah J. McCreary was born and raised in Grand Rapids, Michigan. She is divorced and has a son and five grandchildren. She graduated from Aquinas College, majoring in psychology and sociology. She obtained a Master of Arts degree, as a Family Life Educator, from Western Michigan University and a Master of Divinity degree, at Western Theological Seminary. She is ordained in the Reformed Church in America as a Minister of Word and Sacrament. Deborah has a passion for women and marginalized populations. She has been privileged to serve with various outreach ministries including Rose Haven Ministry, Mel Trotter Ministries, Alpha Prison Ministry, and Degage Ministries. She has preached, led prayer sessions, women's retreats and/or facilitated workshops in Michigan, New Jersey, the Virgin Islands, Chiapas, Egypt, Jordan, and Uganda. She oversees a Reading Mentoring Program at Mulick Park Elementary School that serves over 80 students. Pastor Deborah most recently served as Administrative/Lead Co-Pastor at Eastminster Presbyterian Church. She retired

April 1st, 2023. She in the process of launching her own non-prof-it, Sista2Sista GR so that she may continue walking alongside her sisters in both spiritual and practical life pathways offering retreats, spiritual disciplines, discipleship, family programming, and financial health seminars.

www.ingramcontent.com/pod-product-compliance
Lightning Source LLC
Chambersburg PA
CBHW030402130626
46549CB00004B/1604